The only book you will ever need for Event Planning

By Daniel Melehi

©2023

Contents

Introduction

Welcome to "The only book you will ever need for Event Planning"!

Whether you are a seasoned event planner or just starting out in the industry, this book is designed to be your ultimate guide for organizing successful events. With the rise of online and offline marketing techniques, it has become more important than ever for event planners to have a comprehensive understanding of the strategies and tactics that will help them reach their target audience and create memorable experiences. In this book, we will cover a wide range of topics essential to event planning, including event objectives, identifying target audiences, budgeting, venue selection, event design, marketing strategies, online and offline techniques, social media marketing, publicity, event branding, logistics management, staffing, food and beverage planning, technology solutions, event registration, safety and risk management, creating memorable experiences, evaluating event success, post-event follow-up, and analysis. Additionally, we will examine specific event planning strategies for weddings, corporate events, and non-profit and fundraising events. We will explore the importance of sustainability in event planning and the considerations involved in global event planning and cultural differences. Furthermore, we will discuss the latest trends in the industry to keep you up-to-date with the ever-evolving event landscape. Throughout this book, you will find practical tips, real-life examples, and actionable advice to help you excel in your event planning endeavors. Whether you are organizing a small gathering or a large-scale conference, this book will provide you with the knowledge and tools needed to take your events to the next level. So, grab a pen, get ready to take notes, and let's dive into the exciting world of event planning!

Chapter 1: Event Planning Basics

Event planning can be an exciting and rewarding career. Whether you are organizing a small gathering or a large-scale event, having a solid foundation in event planning basics is essential for success. In this chapter, we will explore the key elements that make up the fundamentals of event planning.

THE IMPORTANCE OF EVENT PLANNING

Event planning is more than just organizing logistics and managing timelines. It involves careful consideration of various factors to ensure a seamless and memorable experience for attendees. A well-planned event can leave a lasting impression, create positive brand recognition, and achieve the desired objectives.

DEFINING YOUR EVENT GOALS AND OBJECTIVES

Before diving into the planning process, it is crucial to have a clear understanding of the purpose and objectives of your event. Whether it is to raise funds for a cause, promote a product or service, or celebrate a milestone, defining your goals will guide all your decision-making throughout the planning process.

Identifying Your Target Audience

Knowing who your target audience is will help you tailor your event to their interests and preferences. Conduct market research, analyze demographics, and gather insights to understand your audience better. This knowledge will enable you to create an event that resonates with attendees and delivers a memorable experience.

Setting and Managing the Budget

Budgeting is an integral part of event planning. It involves estimating costs for various aspects such as venue selection, catering, marketing, and production. Allocating resources efficiently and tracking expenses will help ensure that you stay within budget while still delivering a high-quality event.

Creating an Event Timeline

A detailed timeline is essential to keep track of tasks and deadlines throughout the planning process. Break down the event into phases and create a timeline that includes key milestones, deadlines, and dependencies. This will help you stay organized and ensure that each task is completed on time.

Forming an Event Planning Team

Event planning can be a massive undertaking, and assembling a talented and dedicated team is crucial. Delegate responsibilities, assign roles, and foster effective communication within the team. Collaboration and teamwork are vital for the successful execution of an event.

IN CONCLUSION

Mastering the basics of event planning is the first step towards organizing successful events. Understanding the importance of event planning, defining goals and objectives, identifying the target audience, managing the budget, creating a timeline, and forming a strong team are all key factors to consider. With these fundamentals in place, you will be well-prepared to embark on your event planning journey.

Chapter 2: Understanding Event Objectives

In order to plan a successful event, it is essential to have a clear understanding of the event objectives. These objectives serve as a roadmap for the entire planning process and guide the decision-making along the way.

DEFINING EVENT OBJECTIVES

The first step in understanding event objectives is to define them clearly. Event objectives are specific goals that an event planner aims to achieve through the event. These objectives can vary depending on the type of event and the purpose it serves. When defining event objectives, it is important to consider the overall purpose of the event. Is it to educate, entertain, raise awareness, or generate leads? Each objective will require a different approach and set of strategies.

Examples of Event Objectives

Here are a few examples of common event objectives: 1. Increase brand awareness: The objective here is to promote a brand or organization and create awareness among the target audience. This could be achieved through branding elements such as logos, signage, and promotional materials. 2. Increase sales or revenue: The objective of this type of event is to generate sales or revenue for a product or service. This could be achieved through product demonstrations, special offers, or exclusive discounts. 3. Educate and inform: Some events are designed to provide valuable information and knowledge to the attendees. These events could include workshops, seminars, or conferences with expert speakers and thought leaders. 4. Foster networking and collaboration: Networking events aim to connect like-minded professionals and encourage collaboration and partnerships. The objective here is to facilitate meaningful interactions and create a platform for building valuable relationships.

IMPORTANCE OF UNDERSTANDING EVENT OBJECTIVES

Understanding event objectives is crucial because it provides a clear direction for the entire planning process. When event planners have a deep understanding of the goals they want to achieve, they can make informed decisions about every aspect of the event. By aligning all the event elements with the objectives, event planners can ensure that everything from the venue selection to the marketing strategy supports the desired outcomes. This holistic approach increases the chances of success and helps create a memorable experience for the attendees. Furthermore, understanding event objectives allows event planners to measure the success of their efforts. By setting specific, measurable goals at the outset, event planners can track their progress and evaluate the effectiveness of their strategies. This feedback loop is essential for continuous improvement and future event planning.

CONCLUSION

Understanding event objectives is a fundamental aspect of event planning. By defining the goals they want to achieve and aligning all event elements with these objectives, event planners can create purposeful and impactful events. This understanding also allows for evaluation and improvement, helping event planners deliver successful events time and time again. So, take the time to clearly define your event objectives and let them guide your planning process.

Chapter 3: Identifying Target Audience

Identifying the target audience is a crucial step in event planning. Understanding who your event is intended for will help you tailor all aspects of the event to meet their needs and expectations. By clearly defining your target audience, you can ensure that the event resonates with them and leaves a lasting impression.

WHY IDENTIFY THE TARGET AUDIENCE?

Identifying the target audience is important for several reasons. Firstly, it allows you to customize the event experience and ensure that it aligns with the attendees' preferences. By understanding their demographics, interests, and preferences, you can design an event program that caters to their specific needs. Secondly, identifying the target audience helps in selecting the appropriate venue, marketing strategies, and promotional materials. For example, if your target audience is predominantly young professionals, choosing a trendy and modern venue will likely appeal to them. Similarly, using social media platforms to promote the event will be more effective in reaching this demographic. Lastly, knowing your target audience is essential for setting realistic goals and objectives for the event. Different audiences may have varying expectations and outcomes they hope to achieve by attending the event. By understanding these expectations, you can ensure that the event delivers on its promises and meets the attendees' needs.

HOW TO IDENTIFY THE TARGET AUDIENCE

To identify the target audience for your event, consider the following steps:

1. Conduct Market Research

Start by conducting market research to gather data and insights about potential attendees. This research can include analyzing industry reports, conducting surveys, or studying competitor events. The goal is to collect information that highlights the demographics, interests, and preferences of your target audience.

2. Define Buyer Personas

Based on the market research, create buyer personas that represent your ideal attendees. A buyer persona is a fictional representation of your target audience, including their demographics, interests, behaviors, and motivations. By creating detailed personas, you can better understand your audience's needs and tailor your event accordingly.

3. Consider Existing Customer Base

If your event is targeted towards an existing customer base, analyze your current customers to identify common characteristics and preferences. This information can help you identify similar individuals who may be interested in attending your event. Additionally, reaching out to your existing customers and asking for feedback can provide valuable insights for targeting future events.

4. Use Social Listening

Monitor social media platforms and online communities relevant to your event's industry or theme. Observe conversations and gather insights about the needs, challenges, and expectations of your target audience. Social listening can also help identify emerging trends and topics that can be incorporated into the event to make it more appealing.

5. Analyze Event Data

If you have previously organized similar events, analyze the data and feedback from those events. Look for patterns and trends in attendance demographics, feedback surveys, and registration information. This data can provide valuable insights into the preferences and interests of your target audience.

CONCLUSION

Identifying the target audience is a crucial step in event planning. By understanding who your event is intended for, you can tailor the event to meet their needs and expectations. Conducting market research, defining buyer personas, considering your existing customer base, using social listening, and analyzing event data are all effective methods for identifying the target audience. Taking the time to identify your target audience will increase the effectiveness of your event and create a memorable experience for attendees.

BUDGETING AND FINANCIAL PLANNING

Financial planning is a critical aspect of event planning. Without a well-thought-out budget, it can be challenging to ensure that all necessary expenses are covered and that financial resources are allocated efficiently.

This chapter will guide you through the process of creating a comprehensive budget and developing a sound financial plan for your event.

The Importance of Budgeting

Budgeting is essential because it provides a financial roadmap for your event. It helps you determine the total amount of money you have available and how it should be allocated across various event elements. By establishing a budget, you can ensure that you have enough financial resources to cover all necessary expenses and avoid any unexpected costs. A well-planned budget also allows you to make informed decisions, prioritize spending, and identify areas where you can potentially save money. It helps you achieve your event objectives while maximising your return on investment.

Steps in Budgeting

To create an effective event budget, follow these steps: 1. Determine Your Revenue Sources: Start by identifying all potential revenue sources for your event. These may include ticket sales, sponsorships, exhibitor fees, merchandise sales, or grants. Understanding your revenue sources will help you estimate the total amount of money you have available to spend. 2. Estimate Expenses: Next, estimate the costs associated with each aspect of your event. Consider expenses such as venue rental, catering, audiovisual equipment, marketing materials, staffing, transportation, and insurance. It's crucial to research and gather quotes or estimates from suppliers and vendors to ensure accurate budgeting. 3. Allocate Resources: Once you have determined your revenue sources and estimated expenses, allocate your financial resources accordingly. Prioritize essential elements of your event, such as venue, food, and audiovisual requirements, and allocate the necessary budget to ensure their success.

Consider potential cost-saving measures without compromising the quality of your event. 4. Contingency Planning: It's always wise to include a contingency fund in your budget. This will help cover any unexpected expenses that may arise during the planning and execution of your event. Aim to allocate around 10% of your total budget as contingency to ensure you have a safety net. 5. Track and Monitor: Throughout the event planning process, continually track and monitor your budget to keep it on track. Regularly review your expenses and revenue to ensure that you are within your allocated budget. Make adjustments as necessary to avoid overspending or identify areas where you can reallocate funds.

Financial Planning for Event Success

Effective financial planning involves more than just budgeting. It also includes managing financial resources strategically and prudently to ensure the success of your event. Here are some tips for effective financial planning: 1. Negotiate with Suppliers: When sourcing vendors or suppliers for your event, don't hesitate to negotiate on costs. Often, suppliers are willing to work within your budget or provide discounts, especially if you are a repeat customer or have a strong working relationship. 2. Seek Sponsorships and Partnerships: Sponsorships and partnerships can provide additional financial support for your event. Approach potential sponsors or partners whose target audience aligns with your event's target audience. Offer attractive sponsorship packages that provide value to the sponsors in exchange for financial support. 3. Use Technology for Cost Savings: Leverage technology to reduce event costs. For example, consider using online event registration and ticketing platforms that automate the registration process. This eliminates the need for manual data entry and reduces administrative costs. 4. Evaluate ROI: After your event, evaluate the return on investment (ROI) to determine the success of your financial planning and budgeting efforts. Compare your actual event expenses and revenues against your initial budget. Analyze whether the event achieved its objectives and whether there were any areas where financial resources could have been better allocated. Remember, budgeting and financial planning are ongoing processes. Regularly review and update your budget as new information becomes available or circumstances change. By carefully managing your financial resources, you can create a successful event that meets your objectives while staying within your allocated budget.

Chapter 5: Creating an Event Timeline

Planning and organizing an event requires careful attention to detail and a systematic approach. One crucial aspect of event planning is creating a comprehensive event timeline. A well-structured timeline ensures that all tasks and activities are completed in a timely manner, minimizing the risk of errors or delays.

THE IMPORTANCE OF AN EVENT TIMELINE

An event timeline serves as a roadmap for the entire planning process. It helps event planners allocate resources effectively, keep track of deadlines, and ensure that every aspect of the event is on schedule. A well-defined timeline also allows for better coordination and communication among team members, contractors, and suppliers. Creating an event timeline has several benefits, including: 1. **Organization:** A timeline provides a visual representation of all the tasks and deadlines involved in the event planning process. It helps to keep everything organized and ensures that nothing falls through the cracks. 2. **Efficiency:** With a clear timeline in place, event planners can better allocate their time and resources. They can prioritize tasks, delegate responsibilities, and avoid last-minute rushes or bottlenecks. 3. **Coordination:** An event timeline enables effective coordination among various stakeholders involved in the event planning process. It helps everyone stay on the same page and ensures that tasks are completed in a logical and synchronized manner. 4. **Flexibility:** While a timeline provides a structured framework for event planning, it also allows for flexibility. Changes or unexpected circumstances can be accommodated by adjusting the timeline accordingly, ensuring that the event stays on track despite any challenges.

CREATING AN EFFECTIVE EVENT TIMELINE

To create an effective event timeline, consider the following steps: 1. **Start Early:** Begin creating your event timeline as soon as possible. This allows ample time for adjustments and avoids last-minute rush. 2. **Identify Key Milestones:** Identify the major milestones and deadlines of your event, such as securing the venue, booking speakers or performers, and launching the event marketing campaign. These milestones will serve as anchor points for your timeline. 3. **Break Down Tasks:** Break down each major milestone into smaller, manageable tasks. Assign specific deadlines for each task and ensure that they are realistic and achievable. 4. **Sequence the Tasks:** Arrange the tasks in a logical sequence, taking into account dependencies and interdependencies. This will help ensure that tasks are completed in the right order and no critical tasks are delayed. 5. **Allocate Resources:** Determine the resources needed for each task, including manpower, materials, and equipment. Ensure that resources are allocated in line with the timeline and availability. 6. **Communicate and Coordinate:** Share the event timeline with your team members, suppliers, and contractors. Ensure that everyone is aware of their responsibilities and the associated deadlines. Regularly communicate and coordinate to track progress and address any potential issues. 7. **Monitor and Adjust:** Continuously monitor the progress of the tasks and make adjustments to the timeline if necessary. Be proactive in identifying and addressing any delays or obstacles to ensure that the event stays on track.

CONCLUSION

Creating an event timeline is an essential component of successful event planning. It provides structure, organization, and coordination throughout the entire process. By allocating sufficient time and resources, breaking down tasks, and regularly monitoring progress, event planners can ensure that their events are executed flawlessly, leaving a lasting impression on attendees.

Chapter 6: Selecting the Right Venue

When it comes to planning an event, one of the most important decisions you will make is selecting the right venue. The venue you choose sets the tone for the entire event and can greatly impact its success. In this chapter, we will explore the key factors to consider when selecting a venue for your event.

UNDERSTANDING THE EVENT REQUIREMENTS

Before you can start looking for a venue, it's essential to have a clear understanding of your event requirements. Start by determining the type of event you are planning. Is it a conference, a wedding, a trade show, or a social gathering? Each type of event has unique requirements that will influence the choice of venue. Consider the event size and capacity needs. Will you be hosting a small intimate gathering or a large-scale event with hundreds or even thousands of attendees? Make sure the venue you choose can comfortably accommodate your guest count. Think about the event activities and layout. Do you need a space with multiple breakout rooms? Are there specific technical requirements, such as audiovisual equipment or staging? Understanding these details will help you narrow down your venue options.

LOCATION AND ACCESSIBILITY

The location of your venue plays a significant role in the overall experience for your attendees. Consider the accessibility and convenience for both local and out-of-town guests. Choose a location that is easily accessible by various modes of transportation, including public transportation, highways, and airports. Additionally, ensure that there is ample parking available for those who will be driving to the event. The venue's proximity to accommodations is another crucial factor. If your event spans multiple days or requires attendees to stay overnight, having hotels, inns, or other lodging options nearby is essential. Make sure to research the availability and variety of accommodations in the area before making a final decision.

AMBIANCE AND AMENITIES

The ambiance and amenities of a venue contribute to the overall atmosphere and experience for your attendees. Consider the style and atmosphere that aligns with your event objectives and theme. Is a traditional ballroom setting suitable, or does your event call for a more unconventional or unique space? Take note of the venue's decor, lighting, and acoustics. These factors can greatly impact the mood and experience of your event. Ensure that the venue provides adequate lighting and sound systems to meet your event's needs. If the venue has windows, consider the natural lighting and the view it offers, as it can enhance the ambiance. In addition to ambiance, consider the amenities and services provided by the venue. Does the venue have on-site catering facilities or allow outside catering? Are there dedicated event coordinators or staff members who will assist you with the planning and execution of your event? These amenities can save you time and effort and contribute to a smooth and successful event.

COST AND FLEXIBILITY

Budget is a significant consideration when selecting a venue. Determine your budget early on and factor in all associated costs, including the venue rental fee, service charges, taxes, and any additional fees for setup, cleanup, or security. Consider the venue's flexibility in terms of customization and event setup. Can you bring in your own decorations, equipment, or vendors? Some venues may have strict regulations or preferred vendors, which might limit your ability to personalize the space to match your event vision. Make sure to discuss these details with the venue and clarify any restrictions upfront. Additionally, it is crucial to review the venue's contract and policies carefully. Pay close attention to cancellation policies, deposit requirements, and any penalties for damages or violation of rules. Understanding the terms and conditions will help you make an informed decision and avoid any surprises or unforeseen costs.

SITE VISITS AND REFERENCES

Once you have narrowed down your venue options based on the above factors, it's time to schedule site visits. Visiting the venues in-person allows you to assess the space, ask specific questions, and visualize how it will work for your event. Take note of the venue's cleanliness, maintenance, and overall condition. During your site visit, don't hesitate to ask for references from previous clients who have held events at the venue. Reach out to these references and inquire about their experience working with the venue. Their insights can provide valuable feedback and help you make an informed decision.

Conclusion

Choosing the right venue is a critical step in the event planning process. By understanding your event requirements, considering location and accessibility, evaluating ambiance and amenities, reviewing costs and flexibility, and conducting site visits, you can make an informed decision that aligns with your event objectives and ensures a memorable experience for your attendees.

Chapter 7: Event Design and Theme Development

Event design and theme development are crucial elements in creating a memorable and immersive experience for attendees.

The design and theme of an event set the tone and atmosphere, leaving a lasting impact on guests. In this chapter, we will explore the key considerations for event design and theme development and how they contribute to the overall success of an event.

THE IMPORTANCE OF EVENT DESIGN

Event design encompasses the overall aesthetic and visual elements of an event. It includes everything from the layout and decor to the lighting and signage. Effective event design enhances the overall attendee experience and reinforces the event objectives. Here are some reasons why event design is important:

Creating the Right Atmosphere

The design of an event can greatly influence the atmosphere and ambiance. Whether it's a formal gala, a corporate conference, or a casual networking event, the design elements should align with the intended atmosphere. For example, a corporate event may require a sleek and professional design, while a fun and vibrant theme may be more suitable for a music festival. By carefully considering the desired atmosphere, event planners can create an immersive experience that aligns with the event objectives and resonates with attendees.

Branding and Messaging

Event design provides an opportunity to reinforce branding and messaging. Every visual aspect, from the logo placement to the color scheme, should reflect the event's brand identity. Consistency in design elements helps to create a cohesive and memorable event experience. By incorporating branding and messaging into the event design, planners can effectively communicate key messages and establish a strong brand presence.

Engaging Attendees

Engaging attendees is essential for the success of any event. Event design plays a critical role in capturing and maintaining attendees' attention. Visual elements such as interactive displays, engaging installations, and captivating stage setups can create a sense of excitement and encourage attendee participation. By designing spaces that are both visually appealing and interactive, event planners can create a memorable experience that keeps attendees engaged throughout the event.

KEY CONSIDERATIONS FOR EVENT DESIGN

When developing the design and theme for an event, there are several key considerations to keep in mind. These considerations will help ensure that the design aligns with the event objectives and creates a memorable experience for attendees:

Understanding the Target Audience

Before diving into the design process, it is crucial to have a deep understanding of the target audience. Consider their preferences, interests, and expectations. For example, if the event is targeting a younger demographic, incorporating trendy and modern design elements may resonate more effectively. By tailoring the event design to the preferences of the target audience, planners can create a more personalized and engaging experience.

Aligning with the Event Objectives

Every design decision should align with the event objectives. Whether the goal is to educate, entertain, or inspire, the design elements should support and enhance these objectives. For example, if the objective is to educate attendees, the design may include informative signage and interactive displays. By aligning the design with the event objectives, planners can create a cohesive and impactful experience for attendees.

Choosing a Theme

Selecting a theme can bring cohesiveness and excitement to an event. A theme provides a framework for the overall design and helps create a unified look and feel. When choosing a theme, consider the event objectives, target audience, and industry trends. Themes can range from specific concepts like "Under the Sea" or "Carnival Extravaganza" to broader themes like "Futuristic" or "Vintage Elegance." By selecting a theme that resonates with your target audience and aligns with your event goals, you can create a visually stunning and immersive experience.

Collaborating with Design Professionals

Event design can be complex, requiring expertise in areas such as lighting, decor, and spatial planning. It is often beneficial to collaborate with design professionals who specialize in event design. These professionals can bring a fresh perspective and ensure that the design is executed flawlessly. Working with design professionals also allows event planners to tap into their knowledge and experience, resulting in a more visually striking and engaging event environment.

CONCLUSION

Event design and theme development are critical aspects of event planning. By carefully considering the atmosphere, branding, and attendee engagement, event planners can create a visually stunning and immersive experience that aligns with the event objectives. Understanding the target audience, aligning with event objectives, choosing a theme, and collaborating with design professionals are all key steps in creating an unforgettable event design. By incorporating these considerations, event planners can leave a lasting impression on attendees and achieve their event goals.

Chapter 8: Developing a Marketing Strategy

In the world of event planning, a solid marketing strategy is essential for driving attendance, creating buzz, and ensuring the success of your event. A well-executed marketing plan can help you reach your target audience, generate excitement, and ultimately achieve your event objectives.

WHY IS A MARKETING STRATEGY IMPORTANT?

A marketing strategy is a roadmap that defines how you will promote your event and communicate its value to potential attendees. It outlines the key tactics and channels you will use to reach your target audience and create awareness and interest in your event. A well-developed marketing strategy allows you to: 1. Increase

Attendance: A strategic marketing plan helps maximize event attendance by reaching a larger audience and effectively communicating the value proposition of your event. 2. Build Brand Awareness: A consistent and targeted marketing approach can increase brand awareness and establish your event as a reputable and must-attend gathering among your target audience. 3. Generate Excitement: By creating a buzz around your event through strategic marketing, you can generate excitement and anticipation among potential attendees, encouraging them to register and participate. 4. Drive Revenue: Marketing efforts can directly impact your bottom line by attracting sponsors, exhibitors, and attendees who contribute to the financial success of your event. 5. Enhance Participant Engagement: Through effective marketing, you can engage participants before, during, and after the event, creating a community and fostering long-term relationships.

KEY ELEMENTS OF A MARKETING STRATEGY

1. Define Your Target Audience: Before developing your marketing strategy, it's crucial to identify your target audience. By understanding your attendees' demographics, preferences, and interests, you can tailor your marketing messages and channels to effectively reach them. 2. Set Clear Objectives: Your marketing objectives should align with the overall goals of your event. Whether it's increasing attendance, boosting revenue, or building brand awareness, be clear about what you aim to achieve through your marketing efforts. 3. Tailor Your Message: Craft compelling and persuasive messages that communicate the unique value proposition of your event. Highlight key benefits, such as expert speakers, networking opportunities, or educational sessions, to entice potential attendees. 4. Choose the Right Channels: Consider the best channels

to reach your target audience and create a comprehensive marketing mix. This may include email marketing, social media, content marketing, search engine optimization (SEO), paid advertising, influencer partnerships, and more. 5. Create Engaging Content: Develop high-quality content that adds value to your audience and supports your event's objectives. This could include blog posts, videos, webinars, infographics, podcasts, or case studies. Leverage content marketing to position your event as a valuable resource in your industry. 6. Utilize Social Media: Social media platforms are powerful tools for event marketing. Develop a social media strategy tailored to your audience, and utilize platforms like Facebook, Twitter, LinkedIn, and Instagram to engage with potential attendees, share updates, and create event-related buzz. 7. Implement Email Marketing: Email marketing allows you to directly communicate with your audience and nurture leads. Develop segmented email campaigns to target specific audience segments with tailored messages that align with their interests. 8. Leverage Influencer Marketing: Identify and collaborate with influential individuals or organizations in your industry who have a significant online following. Partnering with influencers can help expand your reach, enhance credibility, and create a buzz around your event. 9. Implement a Content Calendar: A content calendar helps you stay organized and ensure consistent communication leading up to your event. Plan and schedule your marketing activities, including social media posts, blog articles, and email campaigns, to maintain a consistent and timely marketing strategy. 10. Measure and Track Results: Continuously monitor and evaluate the effectiveness of your marketing efforts. Track key performance indicators (KPIs) such as website traffic, email open rates, engagement metrics, ticket sales, and social media analytics. Use this data to optimize your marketing strategy and make informed decisions for future events.

Developing a marketing strategy is a critical component of successful event planning. By understanding your target audience, setting clear objectives, and implementing a tailored marketing mix, you can effectively promote your event, drive attendance, and achieve your desired outcomes. Remember to continuously measure and track results to improve your marketing approach and stay ahead in the dynamic event planning industry.

Chapter 9: Incorporating Online Marketing Techniques

In today's digital age, harnessing the power of online marketing is essential for successful event planning. Online marketing techniques not only enable event planners to reach a wider audience but also provide a cost-effective and efficient way to promote events. In this chapter, we will explore the various online marketing techniques that event planners can incorporate to maximize event attendance and engagement.

UNDERSTANDING ONLINE MARKETING

Online marketing encompasses a wide range of strategies and tactics to promote events through digital channels. These channels include websites, social media platforms, email marketing, search engine optimization (SEO), paid advertising, and content marketing. By effectively utilizing these techniques, event planners can create buzz, generate excitement, and drive attendance for their events.

BUILDING A STRONG ONLINE PRESENCE

Creating a strong online presence is the foundation of successful online marketing for events. Event planners should start by developing a professional and user-friendly event website. The website should include all the necessary event information such as the date, time, location, agenda, speakers, and registration details. It should also have a visually appealing design and be optimized for mobile devices to ensure a seamless user experience.

Search Engine Optimization (SEO)

Implementing SEO strategies is crucial to ensure that your event website appears prominently in search engine results. This involves optimizing your website with relevant keywords, creating high-quality content, and obtaining backlinks from reputable websites. By improving your website's visibility in search engines, you can attract organic traffic and increase event awareness.

Social Media Marketing

Social media platforms play a vital role in online marketing for events. Event planners should identify the platforms that are popular among their target audience and create engaging and captivating content. This can include event announcements, speaker interviews, behind-the-scenes footage, and interactive discussions. Regularly posting on social media, engaging with followers, and utilizing hashtags and influencers can significantly increase event visibility and encourage social sharing.

Email Marketing

Email marketing remains one of the most effective ways to nurture relationships with potential attendees and promote events.

Event planners should develop an email marketing strategy that includes sending out regular newsletters, event updates, exclusive offers, and reminders. Personalizing emails based on attendees' interests and preferences can further enhance engagement and increase event attendance.

PAID ADVERTISING

Paid online advertising allows event planners to reach a targeted audience through various channels such as Google Ads, social media ads, and display ads. By carefully selecting keywords, demographics, and interests, event planners can ensure that their ads are shown to individuals who are most likely to be interested in their event. Paid advertising can be an effective way to generate immediate visibility and drive event registrations.

TRACKING AND ANALYTICS

Measuring the success of online marketing efforts is essential for continuous improvement. Event planners should utilize tracking tools and analytics platforms to monitor website traffic, social media engagement, email open rates, and conversion rates. This data provides valuable insights into the effectiveness of different marketing strategies and allows event planners to make informed decisions for future events.

CONCLUSION

Incorporating online marketing techniques is essential for event planners to maximize event attendance and engagement. Building a strong online presence, implementing SEO strategies, utilizing social media marketing, leveraging email marketing, and utilizing paid advertising are all effective ways to promote events and create buzz. By carefully tracking and analyzing the results of online marketing efforts, event planners can continuously refine their strategies and achieve even greater success in their event planning endeavors.

Chapter 10: Offline Marketing Strategies

Offline marketing strategies are just as crucial as online marketing for successful event planning. While digital marketing methods have become increasingly popular, offline strategies can still effectively reach and engage with potential attendees. This chapter will explore various offline marketing strategies that event planners can utilize to promote their events and maximize attendance.

1. PRINT ADVERTISING

Print advertising remains a powerful tool in event promotion. Placing advertisements in newspapers, magazines, brochures, and flyers can help reach a wider audience, especially those who may not be active online. Event planners can work with graphic designers or marketing agencies to create visually appealing print ads that capture attention and convey key event details. It is essential to choose publications that align with the target audience's interests and demographics to increase the likelihood of reaching the right people.

2. DIRECT MAIL

Direct mail is a targeted offline marketing strategy where event planners send physical mail to a specific list of individuals who may be interested in attending their event. This could include sending postcards, invitations, or personalized letters. Direct mail allows for a more personal approach, helping to establish a connection with potential attendees. Including a call-to-action and a unique discount code can also incentivize recipients to register for the event.

3. OUTDOOR ADVERTISING

Outdoor advertising involves placing advertisements in public spaces such as billboards, bus shelters, and posters. This strategy allows event planners to create visibility and generate awareness among a broader audience. Strategic placement in areas with high foot traffic or near relevant businesses and venues can increase the chances of capturing the attention of potential attendees. Eye-catching visuals, concise messaging, and clear event details are essential for outdoor advertisements to effectively communicate the event's purpose and entice individuals to participate.

4. NETWORKING AND PARTNERSHIPS

Building relationships and partnerships with influential individuals and organizations in the event industry can greatly boost event promotion efforts. Event planners can collaborate with local businesses, industry associations, community leaders, and media outlets to leverage their networks and reach a wider audience. This can include hosting joint events, speaking at industry conferences, participating in trade shows, or sponsoring community events. These offline networking strategies not only increase event visibility but also establish credibility and trust among potential attendees.

5. PUBLIC RELATIONS AND MEDIA COVERAGE

Public relations (PR) is a powerful tool for generating buzz and media coverage for events. Event planners can work with PR professionals to create press releases, media kits, and pitch stories to relevant media outlets. This can include newspapers, magazines, TV stations, radio shows, and online publications. Securing media coverage not only increases event awareness but also enhances the event's reputation and attracts the attention of potential attendees and sponsors.

6. SPEAKING ENGAGEMENTS AND WORKSHOPS

Participating in speaking engagements and workshops related to event planning or the industry in which the event focuses can be an effective way to position oneself as an expert and promote upcoming events. Event planners can offer valuable insights and practical tips during these sessions, leaving a lasting impression on attendees. This can lead to word-of-mouth referrals and increased event attendance.

Incorporating Offline Marketing Strategies into the Overall Marketing Plan

While online marketing strategies offer numerous benefits, event planners should not overlook the power of offline marketing. By integrating both online and offline strategies, event planners can create a well-rounded marketing plan that reaches a wider audience and maximizes event attendance. It is essential to consider the target audience, budget, and resources when selecting the most suitable offline marketing strategies for each event. Regular evaluation and analysis of the effectiveness of each strategy will help event planners refine their approach and continuously improve their marketing efforts. By harnessing the power of print advertising, direct mail, outdoor advertising, networking and partnerships, public relations, and speaking engagements, event planners can generate buzz, increase visibility, and drive attendance for their events. Utilizing a combination of offline and online marketing strategies ensures a comprehensive marketing approach that reaches potential attendees through multiple channels.

Chapter 11: Creating a Compelling Event Website

In today's digital age, having a strong online presence is essential for the success of any event. One of the key elements in establishing this presence is creating a compelling event website. A well-designed and user-friendly website not only attracts potential attendees but also helps in conveying important information about the event and generating excitement. In this chapter, we will explore the steps and strategies involved in creating a compelling event website.

THE IMPORTANCE OF A COMPELLING EVENT WEBSITE

Your event website serves as a virtual hub for all information related to the event. It is often the first point of contact for potential attendees, sponsors, and partners. A compelling event website not only showcases the event's purpose and value but also creates a positive impression and encourages visitors to take action. Here are some key reasons why a compelling event website is crucial:

1. Credibility and Professionalism

A well-designed and professionally crafted event website reflects the credibility and professionalism of the event. It instills confidence in potential attendees and sponsors, demonstrating that the event is organized with care and attention to detail.

2. Clear and Concise Information

A compelling event website provides clear and concise information about the event, including the date, time, location, agenda, speakers, and registration details. It should answer any questions that potential attendees may have and make it easy for them to find the information they need.

3. Engaging Visuals and Multimedia

Visual elements are powerful tools for capturing the attention of visitors. Incorporating high-quality images, videos, and graphics related to the event can create a visually appealing and engaging website. This helps in generating excitement and interest among potential attendees.

4. User-Friendly Navigation

A user-friendly navigation system is crucial for ensuring a positive user experience. The website should be easy to navigate, with clearly labeled menus and intuitive design. Visitors should be able to find information quickly and effortlessly.

5. Mobile Responsiveness

With the rise of mobile devices, it is essential that your event website is mobile-responsive. This means that it adapts seamlessly to different screen sizes and devices, providing an optimal viewing experience for both desktop and mobile users.

KEY STEPS IN CREATING A COMPELLING EVENT WEBSITE

Creating a compelling event website requires careful planning and execution. Here are some key steps to consider:

1. Define Your Website Objectives

Before diving into website design, it's important to define the objectives of your event website. Are you aiming to drive ticket sales, generate leads, or provide information? Clearly defining your objectives will help guide your website design and content strategy.

2. Choose a User-Friendly Content Management System (CMS)

A content management system (CMS) allows you to easily update and manage your website content. Choose a CMS that is user-friendly and offers flexibility in design and functionality. Some popular options include WordPress, Wix, and Squarespace.

3. Craft Compelling Content

Your content should be engaging, informative, and tailored to the needs of your target audience. Use persuasive language and storytelling techniques to convey the value and excitement of the event. Include key information such as the event's purpose, agenda, speakers, and registration details.

4. Design an Attractive Layout

The layout and design of your event website should align with the event's branding and theme. Use visually appealing colors, fonts, and graphics to create a cohesive and immersive experience. Pay attention to the placement of important information and use whitespace effectively to enhance readability.

5. Optimize for Search Engines

Search engine optimization (SEO) plays a crucial role in driving organic traffic to your event website. Conduct keyword research to identify relevant keywords and incorporate them strategically throughout your website content. Optimize page titles, meta descriptions, headings, and URLs to improve your website's visibility in search engine results.

6. Include Clear Calls-to-Action

Calls-to-action (CTAs) guide visitors to take specific actions, such as registering for the event, purchasing tickets, or contacting you for more information. Make your CTAs clear, visually prominent, and strategically placed throughout your website.

7. Test and Optimize

Regularly testing and optimizing your event website is essential for improving its performance. Use tools like Google Analytics to track key metrics such as traffic, bounce rate, and conversion rates. Based on the data, make necessary adjustments to improve user experience and maximize conversions.

CONCLUSION

Creating a compelling event website is a crucial step in your event planning process. A well-designed and user-friendly website helps in establishing credibility, conveying important information, and generating excitement among potential attendees. By following the key steps outlined in this chapter, you can create an enticing online presence that drives engagement and ultimately leads to the success of your event.

Chapter 12: Social Media Marketing for Events

Social media has become an indispensable tool for event planners in reaching and engaging with their target audience. It offers a cost-effective way to promote events, build brand awareness, and increase attendance. In this chapter, we will explore the strategies and best practices for leveraging social media effectively for event marketing.

THE IMPORTANCE OF SOCIAL MEDIA MARKETING

Social media platforms such as Facebook, Instagram, LinkedIn, Twitter, and YouTube have millions of users worldwide. These platforms provide event planners with an opportunity to connect and engage with their target audience on a personal level.

Here are the main reasons why social media marketing is crucial for event success: 1. **Reach a wider audience:** Social media allows you to reach a larger and more diverse audience beyond your immediate network. By creating engaging content and using relevant hashtags, your event can gain exposure to users who may not have otherwise heard about it. 2. **Build brand awareness:** Social media provides a platform to showcase your event brand and create a consistent identity. By sharing compelling content and engaging with your audience, you can establish your event as a reputable and trustworthy brand. 3. **Generate excitement:** Social media offers an opportunity to create buzz and generate excitement around your event. Through engaging posts, teasers, and behind-the-scenes footage, you can build anticipation and generate enthusiasm among your target audience. 4. **Drive attendee engagement:** Social media allows you to interact and engage with your attendees before, during, and after the event. By creating dedicated event hashtags, encouraging user-generated content, and hosting live Q&A sessions, you can foster a sense of community and encourage attendees to actively participate in the event. 5. **Increase event registrations:** With strategic social media marketing, you can drive traffic to your event registration page and increase event registrations. By using persuasive language, compelling visuals, and calls-to-action, you can optimize your social media channels to convert followers into attendees.

KEY STRATEGIES FOR SOCIAL MEDIA MARKETING

To effectively promote your event on social media, consider these strategies: 1. **Define your social media objectives:** Clearly define your goals and objectives for social media marketing. Are you aiming to increase brand awareness? Drive event registrations? Engage with attendees? Having clear objectives will help you craft a focused social media strategy. 2. **Identify**

the right social media platforms: Research and determine which social media platforms are most popular among your target audience. Focus your efforts on the platforms where your prospective attendees are most active. 3. **Create compelling content:** Develop engaging and shareable content that showcases the value and unique aspects of your event. Utilize a mix of text, images, videos, and infographics to capture your audience's attention and encourage them to share your content. 4. **Utilize event hashtags:** Create a unique hashtag for your event and encourage attendees, sponsors, and speakers to use it in their social media posts. This will help in tracking and aggregating user-generated content related to your event. 5. **Engage with your audience:** Regularly interact with your followers by responding to their comments, messages, and mentions. Encourage discussions, ask questions, and foster a sense of community around your event. 6. **Collaborate with influencers:** Identify influential individuals or organizations in your industry and partner with them to promote your event. Influencers can help expand your reach and lend credibility to your event. 7. **Run contests and giveaways:** Organize social media contests and giveaways to generate excitement and encourage user engagement. Offering free event tickets or exclusive access to behind-the-scenes experiences can entice your audience to participate. 8. **Monitor and measure:** Regularly monitor your social media metrics to evaluate the effectiveness of your efforts. Analyze engagement levels, click-through rates, and conversions to make data-driven decisions and optimize your social media strategy.

CONCLUSION

Social media marketing has revolutionized the way events are promoted and has become an integral part of event planning. By leveraging social media platforms effectively, event planners can reach a wider audience, build brand awareness, generate excitement, increase attendee engagement, and ultimately drive event success. Implement the strategies discussed in this chapter to maximize the impact of your social media marketing efforts for your next event. Remember to tailor your approach to each platform and consistently engage with your audience to create a memorable and interactive event experience.

Chapter 13: Publicity and Media Relations

Publicity and media relations play a significant role in event planning by increasing awareness, building brand reputation, and attracting attendees. Effective publicity and media relations can generate buzz, create excitement, and provide valuable exposure for your event. In this chapter, we will explore the strategies and techniques to leverage publicity and media relations to promote your event successfully.

BENEFITS OF PUBLICITY AND MEDIA RELATIONS

Utilizing publicity and media relations can offer numerous benefits for your event. Let's take a look at some of them: 1. **Increased Exposure:** Publicity and media coverage provide an excellent opportunity to reach a broader audience and attract potential attendees who may not have been aware of your event previously. Through media channels such as newspapers, magazines, radio, television, and online platforms, you can extend your event's reach and generate greater awareness. 2. **Enhanced Credibility:** Being featured in reputable media outlets not only expands your event's visibility but also enhances its credibility. Positive media coverage helps build trust and confidence among potential attendees, sponsors, and partners. It validates your event and elevates its reputation in the industry. 3. **Word-of-Mouth Marketing:** Positive media coverage and publicity generate word-of-mouth promotion, which is highly influential and powerful. When people see or hear about your event through credible media sources, they are more likely to share the information with their peers, friends, and colleagues. This organic promotion can significantly increase your event's exposure and attract more attendees. 4. **Networking Opportunities:** Inviting media representatives to your event not only allows for potential coverage but also creates networking opportunities. Building relationships with journalists, bloggers, and influencers can lead to future collaborations and further media exposure for your events.

BUILDING MEDIA RELATIONSHIPS

Forming good relationships with the media is crucial for successful publicity and media relations. Here are some strategies to consider: 1. **Research:** Identify relevant media outlets that reach your target audience. Consider both traditional and digital media, including newspapers, magazines, radio stations, TV channels, bloggers, and influencers. 2. **Create a Media List:** Compile a database of key media contacts, including reporters, journalists, editors, and producers. Include their contact information, beat or area of coverage, and any specific requirements or preferences they may have. 3. **Develop Personal Relationships:** Take the time to understand each media contact's interests and preferences. Engage with them on social media, attend industry events where they are present, and seek opportunities to meet and connect with them personally. 4. **Provide Valuable Content:** Offer media representatives exclusive access, behind-the-scenes content, expert interviews, or early event information. Providing valuable content makes their job easier and increases the likelihood of media coverage. 5. **Be Responsive and Accessible:** Respond promptly to media inquiries and requests for information. Make yourself available for interviews, follow-up questions, and provide resources and visuals to support their coverage.

CREATING A PUBLICITY PLAN

To effectively leverage publicity and media relations, it is essential to create a well-thought-out publicity plan. Here are the key steps: 1. **Define Your Goals:** Start by clearly defining your publicity objectives. What do you want to achieve through media coverage? Examples may include increasing event attendance, promoting specific event features, or building brand awareness. 2. **Identify Key Messages:** Determine the core messages you want to convey through media coverage. Craft compelling and concise messages that align with your event's brand and objectives. 3. **Prepare Press Materials:** Develop press releases, fact sheets, media kits, and any other materials that provide key information about your event. Make sure these materials are professionally written, well-designed, and include engaging visuals. **4. Pitch to Media Outlets:** Tailor your media pitches to each outlet and journalist. Highlight why your event is newsworthy or relevant to their audience. Personalize your pitches and offer exclusive angles or stories to increase their interest. **5. Coordinate Media Attendance:** Invite media representatives to attend your event. Provide them with press passes, access to press rooms or designated areas, and arrange interviews or photo opportunities with key event speakers or participants. **6. Maintain Relationships:** Continue building relationships with the media beyond your event. Keep media contacts updated about future events, industry news, and opportunities for collaboration.

EVALUATING PUBLICITY AND MEDIA RELATIONS

Measuring and evaluating the success of your publicity and media relations efforts is critical to understand the impact and identify areas for improvement. Consider the following metrics and methods: 1. **Media Mentions:** Track and quantify the number of media mentions and articles about your event. Monitor online and offline coverage, including print, broadcast, and digital media. 2. **Audience Reach:** Determine the estimated reach of media coverage by considering the circulation, viewership, or website traffic of each media outlet. Calculate the potential audience reached through media coverage. 3. **Online Engagement:** Monitor social media engagement related to your event and media coverage. Track comments, shares, likes, and mentions to gauge the level of online engagement generated. 4. **Website Traffic:** Analyze website analytics to determine if media coverage has led to an increase in website traffic. Monitor referral sources to identify the impact of specific media outlets or articles. 5. **Attendee Feedback:** Collect feedback from event attendees about how they heard about the event. Include specific questions about media coverage to gauge its influence on attendance. 6. **Media Outlet Relationships:** Evaluate the relationships built with media outlets and individual journalists. Assess the number of ongoing media partnerships or collaborations that resulted from your efforts.

CONCLUSION

Publicity and media relations are invaluable tools for event planners to generate buzz, increase awareness, and attract attendees. By building strong relationships with the media, creating a comprehensive publicity plan, and evaluating the impact of media coverage, you can enhance the success of your event and elevate your event planning efforts to the next level. Remember, effective publicity and media relations are ongoing processes that require continuous effort and attention.

Chapter 14: Sponsorship and Partnerships

In the world of event planning, sponsorship and partnerships play a crucial role in the success of an event. They not only provide financial support but also offer valuable resources, expertise, and enhanced brand exposure. In this chapter, we will explore the benefits of sponsorship and partnerships and discuss strategies for securing them.

WHY SPONSORSHIP AND PARTNERSHIPS MATTER

Sponsorship and partnerships can bring a multitude of benefits to an event. Here are a few key reasons why they matter:

1. Financial Support

Sponsorship provides an opportunity to secure additional funding for your event. Sponsors can contribute to various aspects of the event, such as venue costs, marketing expenses, technology solutions, or even provide cash sponsorships. These financial contributions can help cover costs and ensure a successful event within budget.

2. Enhanced Brand Exposure

By partnering with well-established brands or companies, your event can gain increased visibility and exposure. Sponsors often promote the event through their own marketing channels, which can include social media, email newsletters, website promotions, and more. This exposure can attract a larger audience and create more buzz around your event.

3. Access to Resources and Expertise

Sponsorship and partnerships can provide access to valuable resources and expertise that can take your event to the next level. Sponsors may offer access to their professional networks, industry connections, or specialized skills that align with your event objectives. This can help enhance the event experience and provide added value to attendees.

4. Collaborative Opportunities

Building partnerships with sponsors allows for collaborative opportunities that can benefit both parties involved. These collaborations can include joint marketing campaigns, co-branded content, cross-promotions, or even product/service integrations. By working together, both the event and the sponsor can leverage each other's strengths to create a memorable and impactful experience.

STRATEGIES FOR SECURING SPONSORSHIP AND PARTNERSHIPS

Now that we understand the importance of sponsorship and partnerships, let's explore some strategies for securing them for your event:

1. Identify Potential Sponsors

Start by identifying potential sponsors who align with your event's goals, values, and target audience. Look for companies or organizations that have a natural connection to your event's theme, industry, or target market. Research their existing sponsorships, partnerships, and corporate social responsibility initiatives to gauge their level of interest and potential fit.

2. Craft a Compelling Proposal

Once you have identified potential sponsors, it's important to create a compelling sponsorship proposal. This proposal should highlight the benefits of partnering with your event, including brand exposure, target audience reach, networking opportunities, and any unique selling points. Tailor the proposal to each potential sponsor, showcasing how their involvement can add value to both parties.

3. Develop a Sponsorship Tier System

Create a tiered sponsorship system that offers different levels of benefits and exposure based on the sponsor's investment. This can include different sponsorship packages with varying levels of visibility, branding opportunities, complimentary tickets, VIP experiences, or customized activations. Having a tiered system allows sponsors to choose a level that fits their budget and marketing objectives.

4. Offer Creative Activation Opportunities

Provide sponsors with creative activation opportunities that go beyond the traditional branding and logo placements. Think of unique ways for sponsors to engage with attendees and create memorable experiences. This can include sponsoring interactive activities, hosting branded lounge areas, offering product/service demonstrations, or organizing exclusive networking events. The more customized and tailored the activation opportunities, the more attractive they will be to potential sponsors.

5. Cultivate Personal Relationships

Relationship-building is key when it comes to securing sponsorship and partnerships. Take the time to connect with potential sponsors personally, whether through networking events, industry conferences, or one-on-one meetings. Building a strong rapport can help establish trust, showcase your professionalism, and increase the likelihood of securing their support.

6. Provide Value and ROI

Demonstrate the value and return on investment (ROI) that sponsors can expect from their involvement in your event. This can be done through data-driven insights, attendee demographics, past event success stories, and post-event evaluations.

Showcasing the positive impact of previous sponsorships can give potential sponsors the confidence to invest in your event.

7. Maintain Strong Relationships

Once you have secured sponsorship and partnerships, it's crucial to maintain strong relationships with your sponsors throughout the event planning process and beyond. Keep them updated on event progress, involve them in decision-making where appropriate, and provide post-event reports to showcase the results of their support. By nurturing these relationships, you increase the likelihood of continued support in future events.

CONCLUSION

Sponsorship and partnerships are invaluable resources for event planners. They provide financial support, enhance brand exposure, offer access to resources and expertise, and create collaborative opportunities. By effectively identifying potential sponsors, crafting compelling proposals, offering creative activation opportunities, and cultivating personal relationships, event planners can secure valuable partnerships that contribute to the success of their events. Remember to maintain strong relationships with sponsors and offer value and ROI to ensure continued support in the future.

Chapter 15: Event Branding and Promotion

Event branding and promotion play a critical role in the success of any event. It is essential to create a strong brand identity that resonates with the target audience and effectively communicates the event's value and offerings. In this chapter, we will explore the key strategies and techniques for event branding and promotion.

UNDERSTANDING EVENT BRANDING

Event branding involves creating a unique and recognizable identity for an event. It encompasses the design elements, messaging, and overall experience that attendees associate with the event. A strong brand helps differentiate the event from competitors, builds credibility, and creates a memorable impression. To establish a compelling event brand, consider the following steps:

1. Define your event's unique selling proposition (USP)

Identify what makes your event unique and why attendees should choose it over others. Determine the event's core values, objectives, and key offerings that set it apart from similar events in the industry.

2. Develop a visually appealing event logo and design elements

Create a captivating event logo that represents the event's identity and purpose. Use colors, fonts, and imagery that align with the event's theme and target audience. Consistency in design across all promotional materials, including websites, social media posts, and marketing collateral, helps establish brand recognition.

3. Craft a compelling event tagline or slogan

A tagline or slogan can effectively communicate the event's value proposition in a concise and memorable way. Create a catchy and impactful statement that captures the essence of the event and evokes curiosity or excitement.

4. Develop consistent messaging

Craft a clear and persuasive message that communicates the event's key benefits and unique features. Tailor the messaging to resonate with the target audience, addressing their pain points and desires. Ensure consistent messaging across all promotional channels to reinforce brand identity.

PROMOTING YOUR EVENT

Once you have established a strong event brand, it's time to promote your event effectively. The following strategies can help maximize your event's visibility and attract the target audience:

1. Utilize online marketing channels

Leverage the power of digital marketing to reach a wider audience. This includes creating engaging content for your event website, implementing search engine optimization (SEO) techniques to improve organic visibility, and utilizing email marketing campaigns to nurture relationships and promote the event. Social media platforms and paid online advertising can also be highly effective in driving event registrations.

2. Implement offline marketing tactics

While online marketing is crucial, offline marketing tactics should not be overlooked. Print advertising, direct mail campaigns, outdoor signage, and collaborations with local businesses or industry partners can contribute to enhanced event promotion and increased brand awareness.

3. Leverage influencer marketing

Identify influential individuals or organizations in your industry or target audience and collaborate with them to promote your event. Influencers can help amplify your message, reach a wider audience, and build credibility for your event. This can involve influencer takeovers on social media, guest blogging, or speaking engagements.

4. Encourage word-of-mouth marketing

Word-of-mouth marketing remains one of the most powerful forms of promotion. Encourage your attendees, sponsors, and partners to share their positive experiences and invite others to join your event. Provide incentives for referrals, such as discounted tickets or exclusive perks.

5. Implement a content marketing strategy

Create valuable and relevant content related to your event's industry or theme. This can include blog posts, videos, podcasts, or webinars. Share this content on your event website, social media platforms, and industry-specific forums to position yourself as an industry expert and attract potential attendees.

6. Utilize event partnerships

Collaborate with relevant organizations or businesses to promote your event. This can involve cross-promotion, joint marketing campaigns, or affiliate programs. Partnering with influential brands or industry leaders can significantly increase your event's visibility and credibility.

7. Track and measure your promotional efforts

Set specific metrics to track the effectiveness of your branding and promotional activities. Monitor ticket sales, website traffic, social media engagement, and other key performance indicators. Use this data to identify successful strategies and areas for improvement, allowing you to optimize your future marketing efforts. In conclusion, event branding and promotion are vital for attracting the target audience and ensuring event success. By establishing a strong brand identity and employing effective promotional strategies, you can create awareness, generate excitement, and drive attendee engagement. Remember to consistently communicate your event's value proposition and tailor your messaging to resonate with your target audience.

Chapter 16: Managing Event Logistics

Managing event logistics is crucial for the smooth execution of any event. It involves handling all the details and coordinating various tasks that are essential for the event to run seamlessly. From transportation to venue setup, event logistics play a vital role in creating a memorable experience for attendees.

UNDERSTANDING EVENT LOGISTICS

Event logistics encompass a wide range of tasks, including transportation, equipment rental, venue setup, decor, audiovisual setup, signage, and security. It involves meticulous planning, coordination, and execution to ensure that all elements of an event come together flawlessly. One of the key aspects of managing event logistics is creating a detailed logistics plan. This plan outlines all the tasks and responsibilities associated with the logistics of the event. It includes timelines, budgets, and contact details for all suppliers, vendors, and contractors involved.

CREATING AN EVENT LOGISTICS PLAN

To effectively manage event logistics, it is essential to create a comprehensive logistics plan. Here are some steps to consider:

1. Identify Logistics Requirements

Begin by identifying all the logistics requirements for your event. This includes determining the equipment, furniture, and decor needed, as well as the transportation arrangements for attendees and VIPs. Consider factors such as load-in and load-out times, storage needs, and waste management.

2. Create a Timeline

Develop a detailed timeline that outlines all the tasks and deadlines related to event logistics. This timeline should include dates for ordering equipment, making arrangements for transportation, venue setup, and other logistical tasks. Be sure to factor in time for unforeseen circumstances and contingencies.

3. Coordinate with Suppliers and Vendors

Reach out to suppliers and vendors well in advance to discuss your logistics requirements. This includes contacting transportation companies, rental companies, caterers, and any other vendors involved. Clearly communicate your needs and expectations, and ensure that all contractual agreements are in place.

4. Venue Setup and Design

Work closely with the venue staff to coordinate the setup and design of the event space. This includes determining the optimal layout, arranging for tables and seating, organizing staging and audiovisual equipment, and implementing any special decor or branding elements.

5. Transportation and Parking

Consider the transportation needs of your attendees and plan accordingly. Arrange for shuttle services or provide clear directions for parking and public transportation options. Communicate this information to attendees in advance to ensure a smooth arrival and departure experience.

6. Security and Safety

Ensure the safety and security of your attendees by implementing appropriate measures. This may include hiring security personnel, implementing access control systems, and creating emergency response plans. Consult with local authorities to address any specific safety requirements for your event.

COORDINATING EVENT LOGISTICS

On the day of the event, it is crucial to have a dedicated team in place to oversee the logistics. Assign responsibilities to team members and ensure that clear lines of communication are established. Regular check-ins and updates throughout the event will help address any last-minute issues or changes. Effective communication is key to successful event logistics management. Stay in constant contact with your vendors, suppliers, and venue staff to ensure that everything is running smoothly. Be prepared to adapt and make quick decisions in case of any unexpected situations.

POST-EVENT EVALUATION

After the event, take the time to evaluate the logistics execution. Review what worked well and identify areas for improvement. Collect feedback from attendees, vendors, and staff to gain insights and make adjustments for future events. Remember that event logistics planning is an ongoing process. Learn from each event to refine your processes and continuously improve the execution of logistics for future events.

CONCLUSION

Managing event logistics is a critical component of successful event planning. It requires careful planning, clear communication, and attention to detail. By creating a comprehensive logistics plan, coordinating with suppliers and vendors, and having a dedicated team in place, you can ensure that your event runs smoothly and leaves a lasting impression on attendees.

Chapter 17: Staffing and Volunteer Management

Staffing and volunteer management are essential components of successful event planning. The individuals who make up your event team can greatly impact the overall success and experience of your event. This chapter will explore the importance of staffing and volunteer management, as well as provide strategies and best practices for effectively managing your event team.

1. THE IMPORTANCE OF STAFFING AND VOLUNTEER MANAGEMENT

Staffing and volunteer management play a crucial role in the smooth execution of any event. The individuals you choose to be a part of your event team can greatly impact the success of your event, as they are responsible for executing various tasks and ensuring that everything runs smoothly. When it comes to staffing, it is important to carefully select individuals who are reliable, experienced, and have the necessary skills to fulfill their roles. Whether it is event planners, coordinators, technicians, or other support staff, each member of your team should be competent and dedicated to their responsibilities. Volunteers, on the other hand, are an invaluable resource for event planners. They are often passionate about the cause or event and are willing to offer their time and skills to assist in its execution. While volunteers may not have the same level of experience as paid staff, they can still contribute greatly to the success of your event.

2. STRATEGIES FOR EFFECTIVE STAFFING AND VOLUNTEER MANAGEMENT

Managing your event team effectively requires careful planning, communication, and coordination. Here are some strategies to help you effectively manage your staff and volunteers:

a. Define Roles and Responsibilities

Clearly define the roles and responsibilities of each member of your event team. This will ensure that everyone understands their tasks and will help prevent confusion or duplication of effort. Provide each team member with a written job description and hold regular team meetings to clarify any questions or concerns.

b. Recruit and Train the Right People

When recruiting staff and volunteers, look for individuals who have the necessary skills and experience to fulfill their roles. Conduct interviews or screenings to assess their qualifications and commitment. Provide thorough training and orientation to ensure that everyone understands their roles and knows how to carry out their tasks effectively.

c. Establish Clear Communication Channels

Establish clear lines of communication among your event team. Utilize communication tools such as email, phone calls, or project management software to keep everyone informed and updated on event details. Encourage regular communication and hold team meetings or conference calls to discuss progress, address concerns, and foster teamwork.

d. Delegate and Empower

Delegate tasks to your team members based on their skills and strengths. Trust your team members to carry out their assigned tasks and provide them with the necessary resources and support. Empower them to make decisions within their roles and encourage creativity and problem-solving.

e. Set Expectations and Provide Feedback

Set clear expectations for your team members regarding their responsibilities, performance standards, and expected behavior. Provide regular feedback, both positive and constructive, to help them improve and excel in their roles. Recognize and appreciate their efforts to keep them motivated and engaged.

f. Foster Teamwork and Collaboration

Encourage teamwork and collaboration among your team members. Facilitate opportunities for them to work together, share ideas, and support each other. Foster a positive and inclusive team culture where everyone feels valued and respected.

g. Recognize and Reward

Recognize and reward the efforts of your team members. Acknowledge their contributions publicly, either through verbal recognition, certificates, or small gifts. Show your appreciation for their hard work and dedication, as it will motivate them to continue performing at their best.

h. Address Problems and Challenges Promptly

Address any problems or conflicts within your event team promptly and professionally. If issues arise, listen to all parties involved, seek to understand their perspectives, and work towards finding a resolution. Open and honest communication is key to maintaining a harmonious and productive event team.

CONCLUSION

Staffing and volunteer management are essential for the success of any event. By carefully selecting the right individuals, defining their roles and responsibilities, and effectively managing your team, you can ensure that your event runs smoothly and exceeds the expectations of your attendees. Implement the strategies outlined in this chapter to create a cohesive and high-performing event team.

Chapter 18: Food and Beverage Planning

When it comes to event planning, the food and beverage aspect plays a crucial role in ensuring a successful and memorable event.

Planning and executing a well-thought-out food and beverage strategy can leave a lasting impression on attendees and contribute to overall event satisfaction. In this chapter, we will explore the key considerations and strategies for effective food and beverage planning.

UNDERSTANDING THE EVENT REQUIREMENTS

Before diving into the details of food and beverage planning, it is essential to have a clear understanding of the event requirements. Consider factors such as the type of event, duration, time of day, number of attendees, dietary preferences, and any specific cultural or religious considerations. For example, a corporate conference may require a variety of meal options for breakfast, lunch, and breaks. On the other hand, a cocktail reception may focus more on appetizers and beverages. By understanding the event requirements, you can tailor the food and beverage offerings to meet the needs and preferences of your attendees.

CREATING A MENU

Once you have a clear understanding of the event requirements, it's time to create a menu that will delight your attendees. Consider the following factors when designing your menu: 1. Dietary Restrictions and Preferences: Take into account any dietary restrictions or allergies that your attendees may have. Offer a variety of options, including vegetarian, vegan, gluten-free, and dairy-free choices. Providing a range of options ensures that all attendees can find something suitable. 2. Theme and Ambiance: Align the menu with the overall theme and ambiance of the event. For example, if you are organizing a beach-themed event, consider serving tropical-inspired dishes and refreshing beverages. A menu that complements the event's theme enhances the overall experience for attendees. 3. Seasonality and

Locality: Incorporate seasonal ingredients and locally sourced products into your menu. This not only supports local businesses but also provides fresh and flavorful options for your attendees. 4. Presentation and Visual Appeal: Pay attention to the presentation of the food and beverages. Consider incorporating visually appealing elements, such as colorful garnishes or creative food displays, to enhance the overall aesthetic of the event. 5. Quantity and Variety: Ensure that you offer a sufficient quantity of food and beverage options to cater to the number of attendees. Aim for a balance between variety and quantity to ensure that everyone's preferences are met without over or under catering.

NEGOTIATING WITH VENDORS AND SUPPLIERS

When it comes to food and beverage planning, negotiating with vendors and suppliers is crucial to ensure that you get the best quality at a reasonable price. Consider the following tips when negotiating: 1. Request Proposals: Reach out to multiple vendors and suppliers to gather proposals. Compare the offerings, pricing, and terms to make an informed decision. 2. Discuss Budget and Requirements: Clearly communicate your budget and event requirements to the vendors and suppliers. This allows them to provide tailored proposals and suggest suitable options within your budget. 3. Menu Tastings: Request menu tastings to ensure the quality and taste of the food. This allows you to make any necessary adjustments or changes before the event. 4. Contract Negotiations: Carefully review the contract terms and negotiate any necessary changes. Pay attention to details such as delivery times, staffing requirements, and cancellation policies.

STAFFING AND SERVICE

The quality of service provided by the event staff can greatly enhance the overall food and beverage experience for attendees. Consider the following tips when managing the staffing and service aspect: 1. Experienced Staff: Ensure that your catering team has prior experience in event settings. Experienced staff will be able to handle the logistics and challenges that may arise during the event smoothly. 2. Sufficient Staffing Levels: Determine the appropriate staff-to-guest ratio based on the event's size and requirements. Having enough staff members ensures efficient service and minimizes wait times. 3. Service Standards: Clearly communicate your expectations regarding service standards to the catering team. This includes factors such as presentation, timing, and professionalism. 4. Training and Communication: Provide proper training to the staff members on the event's specific requirements and any special considerations. Encourage open communication channels to address any issues or concerns that may arise during the event.

HEALTH AND SAFETY CONSIDERATIONS

Ensuring the health and safety of attendees is paramount in any event, especially when it comes to food and beverage planning. Consider the following health and safety considerations: 1. Allergen Awareness: Clearly label all food and beverage items to indicate the presence of common allergens. This allows attendees to make informed choices and minimize the risk of allergic reactions. 2. Food Handling and Storage: Ensure that proper food handling and storage practices are followed to prevent contamination and foodborne illnesses. This includes maintaining appropriate temperatures, practicing good hygiene, and handling food in a sanitary manner. 3.

COVID-19 Safety Measures: In light of the ongoing pandemic, it is essential to follow local health guidelines and implement appropriate safety measures. This may include providing individual servings, implementing touchless serving options, and enforcing social distancing guidelines.

CONCLUSION

Food and beverage planning is a critical aspect of event planning that requires careful consideration and attention to detail. By understanding the event requirements, creating a well-balanced menu, negotiating with vendors, managing staffing and service, and ensuring health and safety, you can create a truly memorable dining experience for your attendees. Remember, a satisfied stomach leads to a satisfied attendee!

Chapter 19: Audiovisual and Technology Solutions

In today's digital era, audiovisual and technology solutions play a vital role in event planning. These solutions enhance the overall attendee experience, create memorable moments, and elevate the event to a new level. Whether it's a conference, trade show, or gala, incorporating the right audiovisual elements and utilizing technology effectively can make your event stand out from the rest.

UNDERSTANDING AUDIOVISUAL REQUIREMENTS

Before diving into the world of audiovisual and technology solutions, it's essential to understand the specific requirements of your event. Consider the following factors:

Event Objectives:

What are the key objectives of your event? Do you need to deliver presentations, showcase videos or live stream the event? Understanding the purpose and goals will help you determine the necessary audiovisual equipment.

Venue Specifications:

Take into account the size and layout of the venue. Is it an indoor or outdoor space? Are there any restrictions or limitations on equipment setup? Consider the acoustics, lighting, and visual capabilities of the venue to ensure proper audiovisual delivery.

Audience Size:

The number of attendees will impact the sound and visual requirements. A small conference room may only require basic audio equipment, while a large exhibition hall may necessitate advanced sound systems and projection screens.

Content Delivery:

Consider the type of content you'll be presenting. Will there be slideshows, videos, or interactive displays? Understanding the content delivery methods will help determine the appropriate technology solutions.

SELECTING AUDIOVISUAL EQUIPMENT

Once you have a clear understanding of the event requirements, it's time to select the right audiovisual equipment. Here are some key considerations:

Sound Systems:

Choose a sound system that matches the size and layout of the venue. Consider factors such as microphone requirements, speakers, amplifiers, and mixing consoles. Ensure that the sound quality is clear and audible for all attendees.

Projection and Display:

Select projectors and screens based on the content and venue size. Determine whether rear or front projection is more suitable. Verify the resolution and aspect ratio to ensure optimal visual quality.

Lighting:

Lighting plays a crucial role in creating ambiance and setting the mood of your event. Consider options such as spotlights, stage lighting, uplights, and gobos. Lighting control systems can help create dynamic changes throughout the event.

Interactive Technology:

Incorporating interactive technology can enhance attendee engagement. Consider touchscreens, interactive displays, virtual reality experiences, and augmented reality installations. These technologies can provide a unique and memorable experience for attendees.

Streaming and Recording Equipment:

If you plan to livestream the event or record sessions for future use, invest in professional streaming and recording equipment. High-quality cameras, audio capture devices, and streaming software will ensure smooth delivery to virtual attendees.

UTILIZING TECHNOLOGY EFFECTIVELY

In addition to audiovisual equipment, technology solutions play a crucial role in event planning. Here are some effective ways to leverage technology for your event:

Event Apps:

Developing a custom event app can enhance attendee engagement and provide valuable information. Include features like agendas, maps, speaker bios, networking capabilities, and real-time updates. Utilize push notifications to keep attendees informed and engaged throughout the event.

Online Registration and Ticketing:

Streamline the registration process by utilizing online registration and ticketing platforms. This enables attendees to easily purchase tickets, select sessions, and receive confirmation emails. Use these platforms to collect attendee data, track registrations, and analyze attendee preferences.

Virtual Event Platforms:

Virtual events have become increasingly popular in recent years. Utilize virtual event platforms to host webinars, livestream sessions, and provide interactive experiences for remote attendees. These platforms offer features like chat rooms, Q&A sessions, and virtual networking opportunities.

Event Management Software:

Invest in event management software that streamlines various aspects of event planning, such as ticketing, attendee management, session scheduling, and speaker coordination. These platforms help you stay organized, track important data, and automate repetitive tasks.

Social Media Integration:

Integrate social media platforms into your event strategy. Encourage attendees to share their experiences using event-specific hashtags and leverage user-generated content for promotion. Live social media walls or displays can enhance engagement and create a sense of community.

RFID and NFC Technology:

Utilize RFID (Radio Frequency Identification) or NFC (Near Field Communication) technology to enhance the attendee experience. These technologies can be used for seamless check-ins, cashless payments, interactive experiences, and personalized content delivery.

CONCLUSION

Incorporating audiovisual and technology solutions into event planning is essential for creating impactful and unforgettable experiences. Understanding the specific requirements of your event, selecting appropriate equipment, and utilizing technology effectively will help you deliver a seamless and engaging event. Stay up-to-date with emerging technologies and trends to ensure your events continue to captivate attendees and exceed their expectations.

Chapter 20: Event Registration and Ticketing

Event registration and ticketing play a crucial role in the success of any event. It not only allows organizers to manage attendee information but also serves as a revenue-generating tool and helps in tracking attendance. In this chapter, we will explore the importance of event registration and ticketing, and discuss strategies for implementing an effective registration and ticketing system.

THE IMPORTANCE OF EVENT REGISTRATION AND TICKETING

Event registration and ticketing provide a streamlined process for attendees to secure their spot and gain access to the event. Here are some key reasons why event registration and ticketing are important: 1. Easy Access and Convenience: Offering online registration and ticketing options allows attendees to conveniently sign up and purchase tickets from the comfort of their own homes. This eliminates the need for physical ticket distribution and reduces logistical challenges. 2. Data Collection: Event registration provides organizers with valuable data about their attendees, such as contact information, demographics, and registration preferences. This data can be used for future marketing efforts and to better understand the target audience. 3. Attendance Tracking: By implementing an event registration and ticketing system, organizers can easily track and manage attendee numbers. This information is crucial for logistical planning, such as determining venue capacity, arranging seating, and ordering food and beverages. 4. Revenue Generation: Ticket sales can generate significant revenue for events. By offering different ticket tiers or packages, organizers can maximize revenue while providing attendees with various options to suit their needs and budgets. 5. Communication and Marketing: Event registration platforms enable organizers to communicate with attendees before, during, and after the event. This allows for important updates, last-minute changes, and post-event surveys or feedback requests. It also provides opportunities for targeted marketing efforts.

STRATEGIES FOR IMPLEMENTING AN EFFECTIVE REGISTRATION AND TICKETING SYSTEM

To ensure a smooth and efficient event registration and ticketing process, consider the following strategies: 1. Choose the Right Registration Platform: Selecting a user-friendly and reliable event registration platform is crucial. Look for features such as customizable registration forms, secure payment processing, attendee data management, and the ability to customize ticket types and pricing. 2. Design a Seamless Registration Process: Keep the registration process simple and intuitive. Minimize the number of steps and required fields to avoid overwhelming attendees. Provide clear instructions and make sure the registration form is mobile-friendly, as many attendees prefer to register using their smartphones. 3. Offer Multiple Payment Options: Provide attendees with a variety of payment options, such as credit/debit cards, PayPal, or other electronic payment methods. Consider offering early-bird discounts or promotional codes to incentivize attendees to register and purchase tickets early. 4. Provide Clear Ticketing Information: Clearly communicate the ticket types, pricing, availability, and any terms and conditions associated with ticket purchases. Include descriptions of each ticket tier or package to help attendees choose the option that aligns with their needs. 5. Utilize Scannable Tickets or QR Codes: Use scannable tickets or QR codes to streamline the check-in process and ensure a smooth and efficient entry for attendees. This reduces the risk of ticket fraud and enhances event security. 6. Leverage Analytical Tools: Most event registration platforms offer analytics and reporting capabilities. Take advantage of these tools to track registration and ticket sales, monitor attendance trends, and evaluate the success of marketing campaigns. 7. Provide Excellent Customer

Support: Offer prompt and reliable customer support to assist attendees with any registration or ticketing-related issues. This can be done through email, live chat, or dedicated support helplines. 8. Test the Registration System: Before launching the registration system, thoroughly test its functionality and user experience. Conduct a trial registration process to identify any potential issues or areas for improvement. By implementing these strategies, event planners can ensure a seamless and efficient registration and ticketing process for their attendees. This not only enhances attendee satisfaction but also contributes to the overall success of the event. In conclusion, event registration and ticketing are essential components of event planning. They provide convenience for attendees, valuable data for organizers, and revenue opportunities for events. By implementing an effective registration and ticketing system, event planners can streamline the process and enhance the attendee experience.

Chapter 21: Event Safety and Risk Management

Event safety and risk management are crucial aspects of event planning to ensure the well-being of attendees, staff, and vendors. By implementing effective safety measures and properly managing potential risks, event planners can create a safe and secure environment for everyone involved. In this chapter, we will explore the key principles and strategies for event safety and risk management to help you mitigate potential hazards and ensure a successful and incident-free event.

UNDERSTANDING EVENT SAFETY

Event safety encompasses various aspects, including physical safety, crowd management, emergency preparedness, and risk assessment. It involves identifying potential hazards, implementing preventive measures, and preparing contingency plans to effectively respond to accidents or emergencies. To ensure event safety, it is essential to conduct a comprehensive risk assessment of the venue and all associated activities. This involves identifying potential risks and hazards, evaluating their likelihood and severity, and implementing appropriate control measures. Some common risks and hazards in events include: - Crowd-related incidents such as overcrowding, stampedes, or trampling - Fire hazards, including flammable materials and inadequate fire exits - Security threats, such as terrorism or violence - Health and medical emergencies, including heatstroke, allergic reactions, or accidents - Weather-related hazards, such as extreme temperatures, storms, or natural disasters - Technical issues, such as equipment malfunction or power failure

DEVELOPING AN EVENT SAFETY PLAN

To effectively manage event safety and mitigate risks, it is crucial to develop a detailed event safety plan. This plan should outline the necessary procedures and protocols for handling emergencies, as well as preventive measures to minimize potential risks. Here are some key steps to consider when developing an event safety plan: 1. Identify potential risks and hazards: Conduct a thorough risk assessment of the event venue, activities, and surrounding areas to identify potential risks and hazards. Consider factors such as crowd size, weather conditions, venue layout, and any specific risks associated with the event. 2. Establish emergency procedures: Develop clear and concise emergency procedures that outline how to respond to various incidents, including medical emergencies, fires, security threats, or severe weather conditions. Clearly communicate these procedures to all staff, volunteers, vendors, and participants. 3. Coordinate with local authorities and emergency services: Establish communication channels with local authorities and emergency services to ensure a prompt and coordinated response in case of emergencies. Share your event safety plan with them and obtain their input and guidance. 4. Train staff and volunteers: Provide comprehensive training for staff and volunteers on event safety protocols, emergency procedures, and risk management. Ensure they are familiar with the layout of the venue, emergency exits, first aid stations, and other relevant safety measures. 5. Implement crowd management strategies: Develop effective crowd management strategies to prevent overcrowding, maintain orderly queues, and ensure the safe movement of attendees. This may include implementing crowd control barriers, assigning trained staff members to monitor crowd flow, and establishing designated entry and exit points. 6. Secure the event perimeter: Implement appropriate security measures to control access to the event and ensure the safety of attendees. This may involve hiring security personnel, installing CCTV cameras, conducting bag checks, and implementing access control systems. 7. Provide medical support: Arrange for medical professionals or first aid providers to be present at the event. Ensure that first aid stations are easily accessible and well-equipped with necessary medical supplies. Communicate the location of these stations to attendees. 8. Communicate safety information to attendees: Clearly communicate safety information to attendees through various channels, such as event websites, social media, event programs, signage, and announcements. Include information on emergency procedures, medical assistance, and relevant safety measures. 9. Continuously monitor and evaluate safety measures: Regularly review and update your event safety plan based on feedback, lessons learned, and changes in regulations or best practices. Continuously monitor the event for potential safety issues and address them promptly to maintain a safe environment.

CONCLUSION

Event safety and risk management play a crucial role in ensuring the success and well-being of all stakeholders involved. By implementing effective safety measures, conducting thorough risk assessments, and developing comprehensive event safety plans, event planners can minimize potential hazards and create a safe and secure environment for attendees. Prioritizing event safety not only protects participants but also enhances the reputation of your event and builds trust among potential attendees. As an event planner, it is your responsibility to prioritize safety and take proactive steps to mitigate risks and respond effectively to emergencies.

Chapter 22: Creating Memorable Event Experiences

Creating memorable event experiences is essential for the success of any event. When attendees have a positive and memorable experience, it not only leaves a lasting impression but also increases the likelihood of them attending future events and recommending them to others. In this chapter, we will explore strategies and techniques to help event planners create unforgettable experiences for their attendees.

UNDERSTANDING ATTENDEE EXPECTATIONS

To create a memorable event experience, it is important to first understand the expectations and preferences of your attendees. Conducting surveys or focus groups before the event can provide valuable insights into what attendees are looking for in terms of content, activities, and overall atmosphere. Consider the demographics and interests of your target audience. Are they seeking educational content, networking opportunities, entertainment, or a combination of these? Understanding their preferences will help you tailor the event experience to meet their needs and provide value.

EVENT DESIGN AND THEMING

Event design and theming play a crucial role in creating a memorable experience. The overall ambiance, decor, and visual elements should align with the event objectives and resonate with the attendees. Whether it's a corporate conference, wedding, gala, or trade show, the design should be cohesive and reflect the event's purpose and theme. Consider incorporating unique and interactive elements into the event design. This could include interactive displays, photo booths, themed lounges, or creative seating arrangements. Engaging all the senses through the use of lighting, music, scents, and even taste can also enhance the overall experience.

ENGAGING CONTENT AND ACTIVITIES

The content and activities provided during the event should be engaging and tailored to the interests of the attendees. This can include keynote speeches, panel discussions, workshops, demonstrations, or interactive sessions. Consider incorporating opportunities for attendees to actively participate, such as Q&A sessions, networking activities, or hands-on workshops. Remember to strike a balance between educational and entertaining content. While attendees may be seeking to learn and gain knowledge, it's also important to provide entertainment and opportunities for relaxation and enjoyment. This can be achieved through entertainment acts, live performances, or recreational activities.

PERSONALIZATION AND CUSTOMIZATION

Personalization and customization are key to creating a memorable event experience. As much as possible, try to tailor the experience to each individual attendee. This can be done through personalized communication, personalized event itineraries, or customized swag bags or gifts. Technology can also play a role in personalization. Utilize event apps or registration platforms that allow attendees to create customized agendas, connect with other attendees, or receive personalized recommendations based on their interests. This not only enhances the attendee experience but also provides valuable data that can be used for future event planning.

CREATING WOW MOMENTS

Creating WOW moments throughout the event can significantly contribute to a memorable experience. These are unexpected and impactful moments that surprise and delight attendees. Examples include surprise performances, unique entertainment acts, interactive installations, or VIP experiences. Consider creating unique photo opportunities or immersive experiences that attendees can share on social media. These moments not only create excitement and buzz during the event but also extend its reach to a wider audience.

POST-EVENT FOLLOW-UP AND FEEDBACK

Even after the event ends, the experience should continue. Implement a post-event follow-up strategy to engage with attendees and gather feedback. This can include sending personalized thank-you notes, surveys, or follow-up emails with exclusive content or offers. Feedback is invaluable for continuous improvement. Collecting attendee feedback and analyzing it will help you identify areas of success and areas for improvement in future events. Use this feedback to refine your event planning strategies and create even more memorable experiences in the future.

CONCLUSION

Creating memorable event experiences is crucial for event planners to stand out and achieve their objectives. By understanding attendee expectations, designing immersive environments, providing engaging content and activities, personalizing the experience, creating WOW moments, and gathering post-event feedback, event planners can create unforgettable experiences that leave a lasting impression on attendees. These experiences not only enhance the success of the current event but also pave the way for future events that are even more memorable and impactful.

Chapter 23: Evaluating Event Success

Evaluating the success of an event is essential for event planners to measure the effectiveness of their efforts and make informed decisions for future events. It allows them to identify strengths and weaknesses, assess the event's impact, and determine its overall success in achieving its objectives.

WHY EVALUATE EVENT SUCCESS?

Evaluating event success provides valuable insights that can help event planners refine their strategies, improve future events, and demonstrate the return on investment (ROI) to stakeholders. Here are a few reasons why evaluating event success is crucial: 1. Measure Achievement of Objectives: By evaluating event success, event planners can determine whether they met their objectives. For example, if the goal was to increase brand awareness, they can analyze metrics such as social media impressions, website traffic, and media coverage to gauge the event's effectiveness. 2. Identify Areas for Improvement: Evaluating event success allows event planners to identify areas that need improvement. By identifying strengths and weaknesses, event planners can make necessary adjustments to future events, ensuring continuous improvement and growth. 3. Determine Attendee Satisfaction: Evaluating event success involves gathering feedback from attendees to understand their level of satisfaction. This feedback can provide valuable insights into the attendee experience, including what worked well and areas where improvements can be made. 4. Demonstrate ROI to Stakeholders: Evaluation helps event planners demonstrate the value and return on investment to stakeholders. By analyzing financial data, such as revenue generated and expenses incurred, event planners can provide a clear picture of the event's financial success.

KEY METRICS FOR EVALUATING EVENT SUCCESS

When evaluating event success, it is crucial to consider a range of metrics that provide a comprehensive view of the event's performance. Here are some key metrics to consider: 1. Attendance: The number of attendees is a fundamental metric for evaluating event success. By comparing actual attendance to the target number, event planners can determine the event's reach and popularity. 2. Audience Engagement: Measuring audience engagement during the event, such as participation in interactive sessions, networking activities, and social media interactions, provides insights into the event's level of engagement and attendee interest. 3. Feedback and Satisfaction

Surveys: Gathering feedback from attendees through surveys and post-event evaluations provides valuable insights into attendee satisfaction, preferences, and areas for improvement. 4. Social Media Reach and Engagement: Analyzing social media metrics, such as the number of mentions, shares, likes, and comments, helps evaluate the event's online reach and engagement. 5. Media Coverage and Publicity: Assessing media coverage and publicity generated by the event, including the number of press releases, articles, interviews, and media mentions, helps determine the event's visibility and impact. 6. Revenue Generated: Evaluating the event's financial success involves analyzing revenue streams, such as ticket sales, sponsorships, merchandise sales, and partnerships. Comparing revenue generated to the event's expenses provides a clear picture of its financial performance. 7. Return on Investment (ROI): Calculating the ROI involves comparing the event's financial gains to the investment made. This metric helps event planners demonstrate the event's value and return on investment to stakeholders.

TIPS FOR EFFECTIVE EVENT EVALUATION

To conduct a thorough and effective evaluation of event success, event planners can follow these tips: 1. Set Clear Evaluation Objectives: Define clear evaluation objectives before the event to guide the evaluation process. Determine what metrics and benchmarks will be used to measure success. 2. Use a Mix of Quantitative and Qualitative Data: Gather both quantitative data (numbers and statistics) and qualitative data (feedback and opinions) to gain a comprehensive understanding of the event's performance. 3. Gather Feedback from Multiple Sources: Collect feedback from multiple sources, including attendees, sponsors, speakers, volunteers, staff, and partners. This will provide different perspectives and insights into the event's success. 4. Analyze Data and Identify Key Findings: Analyze the collected data and identify key findings and trends. Look for patterns and correlations to gain a deeper understanding of the event's strengths and areas for improvement. 5. Take Action Based on Findings: Use the evaluation findings to inform future event planning and decision-making. Identify areas for improvement and develop strategies to address them in future events. 6. Communicate Results to Stakeholders: Share the evaluation results with stakeholders, including senior management, sponsors, and partners. Highlight the event's successes and provide recommendations for future events. 7. Continuously Improve and Learn: The evaluation process should be an ongoing and iterative process. Use the insights gained from each evaluation to continuously improve the event planning process and deliver better experiences in the future.

Evaluating event success is a critical step in the event planning process. By measuring the achievement of objectives, identifying areas for improvement, and demonstrating ROI, event planners can continuously improve their strategies and deliver impactful events. Using a mix of quantitative and qualitative data, gathering feedback from multiple sources, and taking action based on findings will help event planners ensure the success and growth of their events.

Chapter 24: Post-Event Follow-up and Analysis

After months of planning and executing an event, it can be tempting to sit back and relax once it's over. However, the work doesn't end there. One of the most crucial steps in event planning is the post-event follow-up and analysis. This chapter will guide you through the important tasks and strategies for effectively evaluating the success of your event.

EVALUATING EVENT SUCCESS

Evaluating the success of an event is essential for event planners. It allows you to measure the achievement of objectives, identify areas for improvement, determine attendee satisfaction, and demonstrate ROI to stakeholders. To effectively evaluate the success of your event, consider the following key metrics:

1. Attendance

The number of attendees is a significant metric for determining the success of your event. Compare the actual attendance against your target numbers and consider factors such as registration rates, walk-in attendance, and no-shows.

2. Audience Engagement

Measuring audience engagement helps determine the level of interaction and interest during the event. This can be assessed through various methods, such as feedback surveys, social media reach and engagement, session ratings, and attendee participation in activities and networking opportunities.

3. Feedback and Satisfaction Surveys

Gathering feedback from attendees is crucial for understanding their overall satisfaction and identifying areas for improvement. Distribute post-event surveys through email or online platforms and ask specific questions about their experience, including the organization, content, speakers, logistics, and overall satisfaction.

4. Social Media Reach and Engagement

Monitor social media platforms for mentions, shares, likes, and comments related to your event. Analyze the reach and engagement metrics to assess the impact of your event on social media channels. Additionally, monitor event hashtags and user-generated content to gauge attendee involvement and excitement.

5. Media Coverage and Publicity

Evaluate the media coverage and publicity generated by your event. Look for news articles, blog posts, social media posts, and any other mentions of your event in the media. Measure the reach and sentiment of these mentions to determine the level of exposure and the overall reputation of your event.

6. Revenue Generated

If your event aimed to generate revenue, measuring the financial success is crucial. Evaluate the revenue generated through ticket sales, sponsorships, exhibitor fees, merchandise sales, and any other revenue streams. Compare the actual revenue against your financial goals and consider the return on investment (ROI).

7. Return on Investment (ROI)

Assessing the ROI helps determine the financial success and efficiency of your event. Calculate the ROI by comparing the total expenses to the revenue generated. This analysis provides valuable insights into the profitability and effectiveness of your event.

TIPS FOR EFFECTIVE EVENT EVALUATION

To make the most out of your post-event analysis, consider the following tips:

1. Set Clear Evaluation Objectives

Before conducting your event evaluation, clearly define what you want to achieve. Establish specific objectives and key performance indicators (KPIs) to guide your evaluation process.

2. Use a Mix of Quantitative and Qualitative Data

Collect both quantitative and qualitative data for a comprehensive evaluation. While quantitative data, such as attendance numbers and revenue figures, provides measurable insights, qualitative data from surveys and feedback allows for deeper understanding and qualitative analysis.

3. Gather Feedback from Multiple Sources

Reach out to all relevant stakeholders involved in the event, including attendees, sponsors, speakers, vendors, and staff.

Consider their perspectives and gather feedback from different sources to gain a comprehensive understanding of the event's strengths and areas for improvement.

4. Analyze Data and Identify Key Findings

Thoroughly analyze the data collected during the evaluation process. Look for patterns, trends, and insights that can inform future event planning decisions. Identify key findings, both positive and negative, and prioritize areas for improvement.

5. Take Action Based on Findings

Use the insights gained from your evaluation to implement necessary changes and improvements. Address any identified weaknesses and build upon the event's strengths. Take proactive steps to ensure continuous improvement in future events.

6. Communicate Results to Stakeholders

Share the results of your event evaluation with relevant stakeholders, including event sponsors, management teams, and other key decision-makers. Present the findings in a clear and concise manner, highlighting both successes and areas for improvement. Use the opportunity to showcase the value of the event and demonstrate your commitment to ongoing improvement.

7. Continuously Improve and Learn from Evaluations

View each event as a learning opportunity and use the insights gained from evaluations to continuously improve your event planning strategies. Incorporate the lessons learned into your future event planning process to enhance the overall success and attendee experience.

CONCLUSION

Post-event follow-up and analysis are vital components of successful event planning. Evaluating the success of your event allows you to measure achievement, identify areas for improvement, and demonstrate ROI. By setting clear evaluation objectives, gathering feedback from multiple sources, and taking action based on findings, you can continuously improve your event planning process and deliver exceptional experiences.

Chapter 25: Trends in Event Planning

Events are constantly evolving, and as an event planner, it's important to stay up-to-date with the latest trends in the industry. These trends not only reflect changing attendee preferences but also offer opportunities to create unique and memorable experiences. In this chapter, we will explore some of the current trends in event planning that you should consider incorporating into your future events.

1. TECHNOLOGY INTEGRATION

One of the most significant trends in event planning is the integration of technology throughout the event experience. From event registration and ticketing to interactive event apps and virtual reality experiences, technology has the power to enhance attendee engagement and create immersive event experiences. Event planners should consider utilizing advanced event management software that can streamline various tasks such as attendee registration, session management, and data collection. By leveraging technology, you can provide a seamless and personalized experience for your attendees while also efficiently managing event logistics.

2. PERSONALIZATION AND CUSTOMIZATION

In today's digital age, attendees expect personalized experiences. Event planners should embrace this trend by incorporating customization and personalization into their events. This can include tailored event agendas, personalized attendee communication, and customized event branding. By making attendees feel seen and valued, you can create a more meaningful and memorable experience. Consider leveraging data and technology to collect attendee preferences and behaviors. This data can then be used to create personalized recommendations, networking opportunities, and session suggestions. Additionally, offering customizable elements such as food and beverage choices, session tracks, and networking events can further enhance the attendee experience.

3. SUSTAINABILITY AND ECO-FRIENDLY PRACTICES

With growing environmental consciousness, sustainability has become a significant trend in event planning. Event planners should actively seek ways to reduce the environmental impact of their events by implementing eco-friendly practices. This can include using recyclable or compostable materials, reducing single-use plastics, implementing waste management systems, and sourcing locally-produced or organic products. Consider incorporating sustainable event design elements such as energy-efficient lighting, water-saving technologies, and eco-friendly decor. Additionally, educate attendees on the environmental initiatives of the event and encourage their participation in these efforts. By aligning your event with sustainability practices, you not only contribute to a better environment but also appeal to socially conscious attendees.

4. HYBRID AND VIRTUAL EVENTS

The COVID-19 pandemic has accelerated the adoption of hybrid and virtual events. These formats allow attendees to participate remotely, providing flexibility and access to a wider audience. Event planners should consider integrating virtual components into their events to cater to both in-person and remote attendees. This can include live streaming sessions, virtual networking opportunities, and interactive virtual platforms. Hybrid and virtual events also offer cost-saving opportunities, as they eliminate the need for large physical venues and reduce travel expenses. By embracing this trend, event planners can reach a global audience, increase event accessibility, and provide unique virtual experiences.

5. EXPERIENTIAL MARKETING

Incorporating experiential marketing techniques has become a popular trend in event planning. Experiential marketing focuses on creating immersive and interactive experiences that engage attendees on multiple sensory levels. These experiences can leave a lasting impact and create positive brand associations. Consider incorporating interactive installations, photo booths, gamification elements, and multisensory experiences into your events. By providing hands-on and engaging activities, you can create memorable moments for attendees and enhance their overall event experience.

6. WELLNESS AND WELL-BEING

As individuals prioritize their well-being, wellness-focused events have gained popularity. Event planners should consider integrating wellness activities into their events to provide attendees with opportunities for relaxation, rejuvenation, and self-care. This can include wellness workshops, mindfulness sessions, yoga classes, healthy food and beverage options, and wellness-focused networking events. By incorporating wellness-focused activities, event planners demonstrate their commitment to attendee well-being and create a more holistic event experience. Additionally, wellness-focused events can attract a specific target audience interested in personal growth and self-care.

CONCLUSION

Staying updated with the latest trends in event planning is essential for creating successful and impactful events. By embracing technology integration, personalization and customization, sustainability, hybrid and virtual events, experiential marketing, and wellness-focused activities, event planners can cater to evolving attendee preferences and deliver memorable event experiences. Stay open to innovation and be willing to adapt to new trends. By doing so, you can set your events apart and leave a lasting impression on attendees.

Chapter 26: Sustainable Event Practices

In recent years, the importance of sustainability has become increasingly evident in all aspects of our lives, and event planning is no exception. Sustainable event practices not only help protect the environment but also contribute to the overall success and reputation of an event. In this chapter, we will explore the importance of incorporating sustainability into event planning and provide strategies and tips on how to organize eco-friendly events.

UNDERSTANDING THE IMPORTANCE OF SUSTAINABILITY

Sustainability is more than just a buzzword; it is a critical consideration for event planners. By implementing sustainable practices, you can minimize the impact of your event on the environment while also creating a positive social and economic impact. Here are a few reasons why incorporating sustainability into your event planning is essential: 1. Environmental Impact: Events often generate a significant amount of waste and consume vast amounts of energy and resources. By adopting sustainable practices, you can reduce your event's carbon footprint, conserve resources, and minimize waste. 2. Participant Expectations: Today's attendees are increasingly environmentally conscious and expect events to be eco-friendly. By meeting these expectations, you can enhance the overall attendee experience and improve your event's reputation. 3. Cost Savings: Sustainable practices can also lead to cost savings. For example, by implementing energy-efficient lighting options, you can reduce energy consumption and lower utility costs. Additionally, using digital communications and registration processes can reduce printed materials and associated costs.

STRATEGIES FOR SUSTAINABLE EVENT PLANNING

Now that we understand why sustainability is important let's dive into some practical strategies for incorporating sustainability into your event planning processes: 1. Conduct an Environmental Audit: Start by assessing the environmental impact of your event by conducting an environmental audit. This audit will help you identify areas where you can make improvements and set goals for implementing sustainable practices. 2. Minimize Waste: Reduce, reuse, and recycle should be the mantra for your event. Implement practices to minimize waste generation, such as using digital invitations instead of printed ones, setting up recycling stations throughout the venue, and opting for biodegradable or compostable materials. 3. Sustainable Food and Beverage: When it comes to food and beverage options, strive for sustainability. Choose locally sourced, organic, and seasonal ingredients that support local farmers and minimize transportation emissions. Also, consider implementing a waste management plan for food leftovers or donating excess food to local charities. 4. Energy Conservation: Optimize energy consumption by using energy-efficient lighting, implementing timers or sensors, and encouraging exhibitors to use energy-efficient equipment. Consider renewable energy options like solar or wind power for powering your event. 5. Transportation and Accessibility: Encourage attendees to use public transportation or carpooling options by providing them with information about available services. If possible, select a venue that is easily accessible by public transportation. Moreover, consider providing bicycle parking facilities to promote greener transportation options. 6. Water Conservation: Implement water-saving measures by using water-efficient fixtures and encouraging attendees to minimize water usage. Provide refillable water stations throughout the venue to reduce single-use plastic bottle waste. 7. Engage Suppliers and Vendors: Collaborate with suppliers and vendors who share your commitment to sustainability. Look for eco-friendly and socially responsible partners who can help you source sustainable products, reduce waste, and support local communities.

EVALUATING AND COMMUNICATING SUSTAINABILITY EFFORTS

Finally, it is crucial to evaluate the effectiveness of your sustainability efforts and communicate them to your stakeholders and attendees. Consider implementing the following practices: 1. Measuring Impact: Track and measure your event's sustainability performance using metrics like energy consumption, waste diversion rate, and carbon emissions. Analyze the data to identify areas for improvement in future events. 2. Certification and Recognition: Explore opportunities to obtain sustainability certifications or accreditations for your event. This can enhance your event's credibility and reputation as a sustainable gathering. 3. Communication and Education: Inform your stakeholders and attendees about your sustainability initiatives. Share your sustainability policy and practices through various communication channels, including your event website, social media platforms, and event materials. Educate attendees on how they can contribute to sustainability during the event. 4. Post-Event Feedback: Gather feedback from attendees and stakeholders to gauge their satisfaction with your sustainability efforts. This feedback can help you identify areas for improvement and demonstrate your commitment to continuous sustainability practices. By implementing these sustainable event practices, you can contribute to a healthier planet, meet attendee expectations, and ensure the long-term success of your events. Sustainability is an ongoing commitment, and as event planners, we have the power to make a positive difference through our actions. Let's embrace sustainability and create events that leave a positive impact on both people and the planet. (Note: Remember to continue writing additional chapters to complete the book)

Chapter 27: Global Event Planning and Cultural Considerations

In today's interconnected world, event planners are often tasked with organizing and managing events on a global scale. Global event planning requires a deeper understanding of cultural differences and the ability to navigate various cultural considerations for successful event execution. In this chapter, we will explore the key aspects of global event planning and the importance of cultural considerations in creating memorable and impactful experiences.

UNDERSTANDING GLOBAL EVENT PLANNING

Global event planning encompasses organizing events that transcend geographical boundaries and cater to diverse international audiences. Whether it's a conference, trade show, corporate retreat, or cultural festival, global events require meticulous planning and attention to detail to ensure a seamless and engaging experience for attendees from different cultural backgrounds. When planning a global event, event planners need to consider factors such as language barriers, communication preferences, cultural expectations, etiquette, and local regulations. Each location has its own unique customs, traditions, and protocols that must be taken into account to create an inclusive and respectful environment.

IMPORTANCE OF CULTURAL CONSIDERATIONS

Cultural considerations play a crucial role in global event planning as they shape the overall experience and influence attendee satisfaction. By understanding and respecting cultural sensitivities, event planners can create an environment that is inclusive, engaging, and enjoyable for all participants. Some key cultural considerations to keep in mind when planning a global event include: 1. Language: Ensure clear communication by providing translation services or hiring interpreters to accommodate participants who may not be fluent in the event's primary language. 2. Etiquette: Familiarize yourself with the local customs and etiquette to avoid any unintentional cultural faux pas. Consider cultural norms around greetings, gift-giving, dress code, and dining etiquette. 3. Religion and Holidays: Be aware of religious holidays or cultural observances that may impact attendance or event logistics. Avoid scheduling events during significant religious or cultural holidays to prevent conflicts and ensure maximum participation. 4. Food and Beverage: Take into account dietary restrictions, cultural preferences, and religious dietary requirements when planning menu options. Provide a variety of choices to accommodate different tastes and ensure that vegetarian, vegan, and allergy-friendly options are available. 5. Event Format: Consider cultural preferences for event formats. Some cultures may prefer more formal, structured events, while others may appreciate a more interactive and informal approach. Tailor the event format to align with the cultural expectations of the target audience. 6. Sensitivity to Cultural Symbols: Be mindful of the use of cultural symbols, imagery, and themes in event branding and marketing materials. Ensure that they are used respectfully and accurately, avoiding any misinterpretations or offensive representations.

BUILDING RELATIONSHIPS WITH LOCAL PARTNERS

When planning a global event, it is essential to establish strong relationships with local partners and stakeholders. Collaborating with local vendors, suppliers, and event professionals who have a deep understanding of the local culture can provide valuable insights and guidance throughout the planning process. They can help with navigating legal requirements, sourcing local resources, and ensuring cultural authenticity in event design and execution. Considerations when selecting local partners include their reputation, experience, cultural sensitivity, and alignment with your event objectives. Building trust and open communication channels with local partners is essential for a successful and culturally sensitive event.

CONCLUSION

Global event planning requires special attention to cultural considerations to ensure that events are inclusive, culturally sensitive, and enjoyable for participants from different backgrounds. Understanding the unique customs, etiquette, language preferences, religion, and cultural sensitivities of the target audience is crucial for creating memorable and impactful global events. By incorporating cultural considerations into the event planning process and building strong relationships with local partners, event planners can deliver exceptional experiences that resonate with attendees worldwide.

Chapter 28: Wedding Planning Tips for Event Planners

Weddings are a special and joyous occasion, but they also require meticulous planning and attention to detail. As an event planner, it is essential to have a comprehensive understanding of the unique aspects of wedding planning. This chapter will provide you with valuable tips and insights to successfully plan and execute memorable weddings.

UNDERSTANDING THE WEDDING INDUSTRY

To effectively plan weddings, it is crucial to familiarize yourself with the wedding industry. Gain a deep understanding of wedding traditions, customs, trends, and etiquette. Stay updated on the latest wedding themes, decor styles, and fashion trends. This knowledge will help you offer personalized and innovative wedding experiences to your clients.

BUILDING RELATIONSHIPS WITH WEDDING VENDORS

Strong relationships with wedding vendors are the cornerstone of successful wedding planning. Establish partnerships with reliable and reputable vendors, such as florists, photographers, caterers, venue owners, and decorators. Collaborate closely with them to ensure seamless coordination and execution of services. Maintain open lines of communication and consistently deliver exceptional service to build a positive reputation within the wedding industry.

CREATING A DETAILED WEDDING TIMELINE

A well-organized and detailed wedding timeline is essential for smooth event execution. Collaborate with the couple to determine the desired wedding timeline, including key milestones, such as engagement photos, dress fittings, rehearsal dinner, and the wedding day itself. Allocate sufficient time for each task, considering potential delays and contingencies. Clearly communicate the timeline to the couple, vendors, and all involved parties to ensure everyone is on the same page.

TAILORING WEDDINGS TO THE COUPLE'S VISION

Every couple has a unique vision for their wedding day. Take the time to understand their preferences, style, and expectations. Collaborate closely with the couple to curate a wedding plan that reflects their personalities and desires. Incorporate personalized details, such as special songs, meaningful decorations, or cultural elements. Pay attention to the couple's love story and incorporate it into the overall theme and narrative of the wedding.

MANAGING WEDDING BUDGETS

Weddings can be expensive, and managing the budget is crucial to avoid overspending and unexpected costs. Work closely with the couple to establish a realistic budget based on their financial resources and priorities. Break down the budget into different categories, such as venue, catering, decorations, attire, and entertainment. Regularly track and update the budget to ensure that expenditures stay within the allocated amounts. Offer cost-saving alternatives and negotiate with vendors to maximize the couple's budget.

COORDINATING WITH WEDDING PROFESSIONALS

Weddings involve numerous professionals, including photographers, florists, caterers, musicians, and wedding planners. As the event planner, it is your responsibility to coordinate and communicate effectively with all these individuals. Maintain a comprehensive contact list of all vendors and professionals involved in the wedding. Regularly update them on any changes or updates, and ensure that all parties are aware of their roles and responsibilities.

ATTENTION TO DETAIL

Weddings are known for their attention to detail, and it is the event planner's duty to ensure perfection. Pay close attention to every aspect, from table settings and floral arrangements to lighting and music selection. Anticipate potential issues and have contingency plans in place. Be proactive in solving any last-minute problems that may arise. Your meticulous attention to detail will contribute to creating a flawless and unforgettable wedding experience.

COMMUNICATION AND COLLABORATION

Clear communication and collaboration are essential for successful wedding planning. Maintain open lines of communication with the couple, vendors, and the wedding party. Regularly update all parties on the progress of the planning process, addressing any concerns or questions promptly. Foster a collaborative and positive atmosphere, encouraging input and feedback from all involved. Effective communication and collaboration ensure that everyone is working towards the same goal of creating a memorable wedding day.

REMAINING CALM UNDER PRESSURE

Weddings can be emotionally charged events, and it is important for event planners to remain calm and composed throughout the process. Stressful situations may arise, such as last-minute changes, unforeseen challenges, or emotional outbursts. In these moments, it is crucial to maintain professionalism, problem-solving skills, and a positive attitude. Your ability to handle pressure gracefully will set the tone for a smooth and enjoyable wedding day.

ENSURING A MEMORABLE GUEST EXPERIENCE

A successful wedding goes beyond meeting the couple's expectations; it also involves creating a memorable experience for the guests. Consider their comfort, entertainment, and overall enjoyment. Pay attention to details such as seating arrangements, guest favors, and personalized touches. Plan engaging activities and surprises that will leave a lasting impression on the guests, ensuring that they have an unforgettable time celebrating the couple's special day.

Incorporating Wedding Trends

To stay relevant and appeal to modern couples, it is important to be aware of the latest wedding trends. Stay updated on popular wedding themes, color palettes, menu trends, and entertainment options. Incorporate these trends into your wedding planning services, offering couples fresh and innovative ideas that align with their vision. Be creative and willing to explore new concepts to create truly memorable weddings.

Conclusion

Wedding planning requires a unique set of skills and attention to detail. As an event planner, understanding the wedding industry, building strong vendor relationships, creating detailed timelines, and tailoring weddings to the couple's vision are essential. Effective communication, remaining calm under pressure, and ensuring a memorable guest experience will contribute to your success in the wedding planning industry. Stay updated on wedding trends to offer fresh and innovative ideas that will make each wedding a beautiful and unforgettable celebration of love.

Chapter 29: Corporate Event Planning Strategies

Corporate events play a significant role in the business world. They serve as opportunities for companies to showcase their products or services, connect with their target audience, enhance brand recognition, network with industry professionals, and even generate leads and sales. Planning and executing successful corporate events requires careful consideration of various strategies. In this chapter, we will explore some effective corporate event planning strategies that event planners can employ to ensure the success of their events.

UNDERSTANDING CORPORATE EVENT OBJECTIVES

The first step in planning any corporate event is to understand the objectives that the company aims to achieve. Corporate events can serve various purposes such as: 1. Product Launch: Introducing new products or services to the market and creating buzz and excitement among attendees. 2. Networking and Collaboration: Creating opportunities for attendees to connect, network, and collaborate with industry professionals and potential partners. 3. Training and Education: Providing educational sessions, workshops, or seminars to enhance the attendees' knowledge and skills. 4. Brand Awareness and Promotion: Increasing brand recognition and promoting the company's products, services, or values to a targeted audience. 5. Employee Engagement and Appreciation: Celebrating achievements, recognizing employees' efforts, and fostering a positive company culture. Understanding the specific objectives of the corporate event will guide the event planning process and help event planners make informed decisions regarding event design, marketing strategies, and attendee engagement.

TARGET AUDIENCE AND PERSONALIZATION

Identifying and understanding the target audience is crucial for corporate event planning. Different corporate events may cater to diverse groups, such as clients, business partners, industry professionals, or employees. Event planners need to customize the event experience to meet the needs and preferences of these different target audiences. This includes considering factors like demographics, professional backgrounds, and interests. Personalization is a key strategy to make corporate events more engaging and memorable for attendees. Event planners can leverage attendee data to create tailored experiences, such as personalized agendas, customized event branding, or targeted communication. Personalization can also extend to the event program, incorporating sessions or workshops that cater specifically to the interests of different segments of the audience.

STRATEGIC EVENT DESIGN

Event design and aesthetics play a vital role in corporate events. The design should align with the objectives and branding of the company hosting the event. Event planners should consider the following when designing the event: 1. Theme and Branding: Develop a cohesive theme and incorporate the company's branding elements throughout the event, including signage, decorations, and marketing materials. 2. Venue Selection: Choose a venue that aligns with the event objectives and desired atmosphere. The venue should have the necessary facilities and amenities to accommodate the event's requirements. 3. Set Design and Stage Setup: Create an engaging stage setup and set design that enhances the event's overall ambiance and reinforces the event's messaging. 4. Audiovisual and Lighting: Employ appropriate audiovisual equipment and lighting to create a visually stimulating and immersive experience for attendees. 5. Interactive Elements: Incorporate interactive elements such as touchscreens, virtual reality experiences, or gamification to elevate attendee engagement and create memorable experiences.

ENGAGING CONTENT AND EFFECTIVE PRESENTATIONS

Corporate events often include presentations, panel discussions, or workshops. To keep attendees engaged and interested, event planners should focus on developing compelling content and structuring effective presentations. Key strategies include: 1. Engaging Speakers:

Invite industry experts or inspirational speakers who are knowledgeable and captivating to deliver compelling presentations. 2. Interactive Sessions: Incorporate interactive elements, such as live polls, Q&A sessions, or breakout groups, to encourage active participation from attendees. 3. Visual Presentations: Utilize striking visuals, multimedia content, and storytelling techniques to make presentations more engaging and memorable. 4. Varied Formats: Offer a mix of presentation formats, including panel discussions, fireside chats, or workshops, to cater to different learning preferences and maintain attendee interest. 5. Networking Opportunities: Create dedicated networking sessions or activities that allow attendees to connect with peers and industry professionals, fostering collaboration and relationship-building opportunities.

EFFECTIVE NETWORKING AND RELATIONSHIP BUILDING

Corporate events present valuable networking opportunities for attendees. To maximize these opportunities, event planners should consider the following strategies: 1. Pre-event Communication: Foster attendee engagement and facilitate networking before the event by providing access to event apps or online communities where participants can connect and start conversations. 2. Facilitated Networking: Organize structured networking sessions, such as speed networking or roundtable discussions, where attendees can meet and interact with other professionals in a meaningful way. 3. Engaging Activities: Incorporate interactive and social activities, such as team-building exercises or icebreaker games, to encourage attendees to connect and build relationships in a more relaxed setting. 4. Personalized Recommendations: Leverage attendee data to provide personalized recommendations for networking connections, matching attendees with complementary interests or backgrounds. 5. Post-event Follow-up: Encourage attendees to maintain connections after the event by providing contact information and resources to help them stay in touch with new contacts.

MEASURING SUCCESS AND CONTINUOUS IMPROVEMENT

Measuring the success of a corporate event is crucial for event planners to evaluate the effectiveness of their strategies and make informed decisions for future events. Some metrics to consider when measuring success include: 1. Attendance and Registrations: Measure the number of registrations and actual attendee turnout to assess the event's popularity and reach. 2. Attendee Satisfaction: Gather feedback from attendees through post-event surveys to evaluate their satisfaction with the event experience. 3. Social Media Engagement:

Monitor social media metrics such as likes, shares, and comments to gauge attendee engagement and online buzz generated by the event. 4. Lead Generation and Conversion: Measure the number of leads generated and track their conversion into prospects or sales to determine the event's impact on business objectives. 5. Return on Investment (ROI): Evaluate the financial performance of the event by comparing the costs incurred with the revenue generated or business outcomes achieved. By analyzing these metrics and insights, event planners can identify areas of improvement, refine their strategies, and deliver more successful corporate events in the future.

CONCLUSION

Corporate event planning requires careful consideration of various strategies to ensure the event's success. Event planners should focus on understanding the event objectives, customizing the event experience to the target audience, implementing a strategic event design, creating engaging content and effective presentations, facilitating networking and relationship building, and measuring the event's success for continuous improvement. By implementing these strategies, event planners can create memorable and impactful corporate events that achieve the desired objectives and enhance the company's reputation and brand recognition.

Chapter 30: Non-Profit and Fundraising Event Planning

Non-profit organizations rely on fundraising events to raise awareness and generate financial support for their causes. Planning and executing successful non-profit and fundraising events involves specific considerations and strategies. In this chapter, we will explore the key aspects of non-profit and fundraising event planning, including understanding the mission and goals, creating compelling messaging, engaging donors, maximizing revenue generation, and evaluating the success of the event.

UNDERSTANDING THE MISSION AND GOALS

Before planning a non-profit or fundraising event, it is essential to have a clear understanding of the organization's mission and goals. This understanding will guide the event planning process and ensure that the event aligns with the organization's purpose. It is important to consider the target audience, the cause or issue being supported, and the desired outcomes of the event.

CREATING COMPELLING MESSAGING

Effective messaging is crucial for non-profit and fundraising events to attract donors and generate support. The messaging should clearly communicate the organization's mission and impact, as well as inspire attendees to take action. This can be achieved through powerful storytelling, highlighting success stories, and conveying the urgency and importance of the cause. Utilizing both traditional and digital marketing channels can help amplify the messaging and reach a wider audience.

ENGAGING DONORS

Engaging donors is a key component of non-profit and fundraising event planning. Building strong relationships with current and prospective donors is essential for long-term support. This can be achieved through personalized communication, providing regular updates on the organization's activities and impact, and recognizing and showing gratitude for donors' contributions. Donor engagement strategies include hosting donor appreciation events, involving donors in the planning process, and providing opportunities for involvement and volunteerism.

MAXIMIZING REVENUE GENERATION

Generating revenue is a primary objective of non-profit and fundraising events. It is important to consider various revenue streams, including ticket sales, sponsorships, auctions, donations, and grant opportunities. Creating an effective fundraising plan and implementing innovative fundraising strategies can help maximize revenue generation. This can include offering unique experiences and incentives to attendees, partnering with local businesses for in-kind donations and support, and leveraging technology for online fundraising campaigns.

EVALUATING THE SUCCESS OF THE EVENT

Evaluating the success of a non-profit or fundraising event is crucial for future planning and improvement. Key metrics to consider include the amount of funds raised, donor retention rate, attendee satisfaction, and the impact of the event on the organization's mission. Collecting feedback from attendees, volunteers, and donors through surveys or interviews can provide valuable insights. Evaluating the effectiveness of the event's marketing and communication strategies is also important for refining future event planning efforts. Non-profit and fundraising event planning require careful consideration of the organization's mission and goals, creating compelling messaging, engaging donors, maximizing revenue generation, and evaluating the success of the event. By following these strategies and effectively coordinating all aspects of the event, non-profit organizations can create impactful events that generate support and raise awareness for their causes.

Conclusion

Congratulations! You have now completed the journey through "The Only Book You Will Ever Need for Event Planning." Throughout this book, we have explored the essential elements and strategies for successful event planning, both online and offline. We have learned that event planning involves careful consideration of various factors, and well-planned events not only leave a lasting impression but also achieve their objectives. In the beginning, we discussed the basics of event planning and the importance of understanding event objectives. Defining these objectives serves as a roadmap for the planning process, helps make informed decisions, and allows for measuring the success of efforts. Identifying the target audience is another crucial aspect of event planning. Tailoring the event experience to meet attendees' needs and preferences ensures maximum engagement and satisfaction. Through market research, defining buyer personas, analyzing data, and utilizing social listening, we can gain valuable insights into our target audience. Financial planning is a cornerstone of event planning as it provides a roadmap and ensures that expenses are covered. We discussed budgeting, negotiating with suppliers, seeking sponsorships and partnerships, and using technology for cost-saving opportunities. Creating a detailed event timeline is essential for organization and coordination. It helps keep tasks on schedule, ensures efficient execution, and facilitates effective communication among team members, contractors, and suppliers. Selecting the right venue is critical to the success of an event. We explored factors to consider such as event requirements, location, ambiance, cost, and conducted site visits to aid in making an informed decision. Developing a marketing strategy is key to driving attendance and ensuring event success. By defining the target audience, setting clear objectives, tailoring the message, and choosing the right channels, we can create engaging content, utilize social media and email marketing, and measure and track results. We then delved into online and offline marketing strategies. Online marketing techniques such as websites, social media, email marketing, and paid advertising, combined with offline tactics like print advertising, direct mail, outdoor advertising, and partnerships, help reach a wider audience and build brand awareness. A compelling event website is essential in today's digital age. We explored the importance of credibility, clear information, engaging visuals, user-friendly navigation, and mobile responsiveness. Social media marketing has revolutionized event promotion. By defining objectives, choosing the right platforms, creating compelling content, and engaging with the audience, we can maximize reach, build excitement, and increase event registrations. Publicity and media relations play a crucial role in event planning. By building media relationships, creating a publicity plan, and evaluating success through media mentions, audience reach, online engagement, and attendee feedback, we can enhance exposure and credibility. Sponsorship and partnerships are vital for successful events. We discussed strategies for securing sponsorships and partnerships, cultivating relationships, providing value and ROI, and maintaining strong connections. Event branding and promotion help create a unique identity and generate excitement. Through unique selling propositions, visually appealing design elements, consistent messaging, and targeted promotion, we can maximize event exposure and attendee engagement. Managing event logistics involves careful planning and coordination. By identifying requirements, creating a detailed plan, communicating with suppliers and vendors, and evaluating execution, we can ensure smooth operations and a seamless event experience. Staffing and volunteer management are crucial for event success.

Defining roles and responsibilities, recruiting and training the right people, empowering team members, and fostering teamwork are key strategies for effective management. Food and beverage planning should be carefully considered to leave a lasting impression on attendees. By understanding event requirements, creating menus, negotiating with vendors, and managing staffing and service, we can ensure a memorable dining experience. Audiovisual and technology solutions help create impactful event experiences. By understanding requirements, selecting appropriate equipment, and utilizing technology effectively, we can surpass attendee expectations and deliver unforgettable moments. Event registration and ticketing systems are essential for easy access, data collection, communication, and revenue generation. By implementing a seamless registration process, offering multiple payment options, and providing excellent customer support, we can enhance the attendee experience. Event safety and risk management are crucial for the well-being of all stakeholders. By identifying potential risks, establishing emergency procedures, coordinating with local authorities, and continuously evaluating safety measures, we can ensure a secure and enjoyable event. Creating memorable event experiences is a key objective of event planners. By understanding attendee expectations, incorporating engaging content and activities, personalizing the event, and following up with attendees, we can leave a lasting impression. Evaluating event success allows for continuous improvement. By measuring metrics such as attendance, engagement, feedback, social media reach, media coverage, revenue generation, and ROI, we can identify areas for improvement and refine our strategies. Post-event follow-up and analysis provide valuable insights. By setting clear evaluation objectives, gathering feedback from multiple sources, analyzing data, and taking action based on findings, we can continuously improve and learn from each event. We also explored trends in event planning, such as technology integration, personalization and customization, sustainability practices, hybrid and virtual events, experiential marketing, and wellness and well-being initiatives. Embracing these trends allows event planners to stay ahead and deliver exceptional experiences. Lastly, we discussed global event planning and cultural considerations. Understanding cultural differences, language barriers, communication preferences, etiquette, and local regulations helps create inclusive and impactful events. We also touched upon wedding planning tips for event planners and strategies for corporate, non-profit, and fundraising event planning, highlighting the importance of customization, attention to detail, coordination, and effective communication. In conclusion, event planning is a multifaceted endeavor that requires meticulous attention to detail, strategic thinking, creativity, and effective execution. By mastering the foundational elements covered in this book, event planners can ensure successful events that leave a lasting impression on attendees and achieve their objectives. Remember, continuous learning and adaptation to industry trends are key to staying ahead in the dynamic world of event planning. Thank you for joining us on this event planning journey. We wish you the best of luck in all your future endeavors and hope that "The Only Book You Will Ever Need for Event Planning" serves as a valuable resource throughout your career. Happy planning!